FINANCE AT 21

MASTERING PERSONAL FINANCE WHEN YOU BEGIN YOUR CAREER

JANVI DHABALIA

ISBN 979-8-89133-355-0

*To my mom and dad
for encouraging me to be the best at what I do.*

CONTENTS

ACKNOWLEDGEMENTS

This book is a product of collaborative synergy!

I firmly hold the belief that extraordinary success is never an individual's achievement. It is the collective strength of a great team that paves the way for success. With immense gratitude, I would like to extend my heartfelt thanks to my dedicated team for their invaluable contribution in effectively translating my thoughts into the pages of this book.

My special thanks to my grandparents (Jayantilal & Rama Dhabalia), mom (Jigna Dhabalia), dad (Deepak Dhabalia), uncle (Jignesh Dhabalia), aunt (Arti Dhabalia) and sisters (Priya & Shakshi) for supporting me throughout my journey of writing this book and mainly, for making me so capable of becoming an author. My rock solid family is truly the backbone of every achievement.

To my mentors who opened and expanded my vision at every stage of life and allowed me to be a student of your expertise - Vijayalakshmi Suvarna, Santosh Nair, Jagdish Joshi, Amol Muley, Dr. Jitendra Adhia, Dr. Shilpa Desai.

Prof. Vijayalakshmi Suvarna, hats off to you for picking out my strength and pushing me to author a book. You have been my greatest inspiration.

To my teachers who helped me improve my vocabulary and writing skills - Sunita Pandya and Johana Braganza. A special thanks to Trinity School Of London institution too for all the elocution examinations.

I am also grateful to D.G. Khetan International School, Utpal Shanghvi Global School and Indian School Of Management and Entrepreneurship for being my best teachers and companions during my growing up years.

My dedicated team at DD's Real Wealth Maximizer also did a phenomenal job of taking up most of my responsibilities at work, so that I could focus on bringing out the best in this book.

Thank you to my friends for standing by me throughout my authoring journey.

To my publisher, Notion Press and it's great team who patiently helped me publish my book. Sayoni and Saransh - my sincere thanks to you.

And finally, to Maanav, for his unwavering love and steadfast support.

NOTE FROM DEEPAK DHABALIA

As your father, I have watched you grow, learn, and achieve incredible milestones in your life. Today, I am bursting with pride and joy as I hold in my hands the book you've written, a masterpiece on mastering personal finance at the start of one's career.

I remember our conversations about the importance of financial responsibility and how you always sought to understand the nuances of money management. Now, you've taken that knowledge and turned it into a guide that will undoubtedly change the lives of every individual who reads this book. Your mantra, "Financial freedom is within reach for all," resonates deeply, even in this book.

This book is not only a reflection of your immense learnings from all the mentors but also your compassion. You've made complex financial concepts accessible to everyone, ensuring that your readers can make informed choices about their finances. Your words will inspire many to take control of their financial destinies.

Your mission to guide 1 lakh individuals to achieve financial freedom is evident on every page of this book. It's not just a showcase of what you know; it's a reflection of your sincere desire to give others the knowledge they need to manage their money wisely.

As your father, I've always believed in your potential, and today, you've exceeded my expectations. I am honored to be your father and to witness your incredible journey.

With all my love and admiration,
India's Leading Money Mastery Coach
Deepak Dhabalia

SPECIAL MESSAGE FROM PROFESSOR VIJAYALAKSHMI SUVARNA

If you are over 40, the first reaction you will have when you read this book is anger at Janvi because she wasn't there to guide you a couple of decades back. And if you are in your 20s, you will love her for guiding you now. This book will do what your parents, teachers, friends, and colleagues have been unable to do. It will change your mind, mindset, and attitude toward saving, spending, investing, gaining, losing, winning, and patience.

I have known Janvi since the time she was a child, scurrying around during training programs and events with her father. Her energy was infectious then, and it hasn't waned now. Though her formal and advanced education might have started after 20, she is like the proverbial 'Abhimanyu' who started learning in his mother's womb. In this case, it was her father's office from the time she was an infant. And all that wisdom and understanding of the role that money plays in your life as a youth will be evident in this book.

This book is iconic because never before has someone so young written in such depth and detail about this fascinating topic. And I believe that live news is always more relevant than historical retrospection. So, you will not get the knowledge that you seek in this book as a 'has-been' and 'done-that.' Rather, you will get ideas on 'is-being' and 'doing-that' right from the horse's mouth. This means that if you are in your twenties, this book is 100% implementable for you. Isn't that great? Most books speak about stuff that you 'should have done.' There are no 'if only (s)' in this book. It gives you the bandwidth to start your investment and saving journey even if you just get pocket money today.

Every word in this book is entirely Janvi's, but every thought in this book is garnered from the great minds that have created uncountable wealth all across the world. She has read, absorbed, modified, and innovated world-class thoughts on wealth creation to make it completely relevant and applicable to you, the young reader.

I wish I had had someone like Janvi to guide me on my wealth creation journey when I was in my 20s. I would not have taken 2 decades to experience prosperity then. I would have had more clarity about my life, my goals, my responsibilities, and my lifestyle.

I promise you that this book is a great read, and you won't be satisfied by reading it just once. You will want to read it again and again and want to share it with your children, siblings, friends, and even parents.

And with every phrase that resonates with you, you will bless Janvi. Just like I do...

Vijayee Bhava
Vijayalakshmi Suvarna
MD – Liberation Coaches Pvt. Ltd.
Empowerment Coach to Janvi Dhabalia

TESTIMONIALS

1. Meena Desai

I wanted to extend my heartfelt congratulations to you on your remarkable achievement of writing your debut book on financial literacy! Your dedication and commitment to this project have truly shone through, and I am incredibly proud of your accomplishments.

Your sincerity and passion for finance and entrepreneurship have been evident throughout your journey with us at ISME, the School of Management and Entrepreneurship, where you pursued your undergraduate studies. Your in-depth knowledge and genuine interest in these subjects have undoubtedly enriched the content of your book. It's inspiring to see your enthusiasm for spreading financial literacy and empowering others to take control of their financial futures.

I have no doubt that your book will serve as a valuable resource for many individuals seeking to improve their financial literacy and embark on entrepreneurial endeavors. Your hard work and determination are testaments to what can be achieved through perseverance and a strong sense of purpose.

Once again, congratulations on this outstanding achievement. I look forward to witnessing the positive impact your book will undoubtedly have on the lives of its readers.

Meena Desai
Director, Undergraduate Programs
ATLAS SkillTech University
Mumbai

2. Himani

I am someone who loves connecting with people, and I am extremely passionate about my work. A motivational speaker, a life coach, and a corporate trainer, I have transformed lives, but I was always weak in managing my money. I have known Janvi since she was in her teens, but I have also seen her do wonders in her career, ever since she started guiding me with my finances. Her command over this subject is brilliant, and I know she is the best person to write this book. I am sure this book has all your answers related to personal finance.

Himani
Founder of Himani's Happiness Hub

3. Dr. Umang Gosalia

I started planning my personal finances with Janvi one and a half years ago, and to my surprise, this Young Champ has made a drastic difference in the way I look at money. Not just as a medium of exchange, but as a positive energy that needs to be treated like my best friend—that's how I look at money now.

Currently, I am in my late thirties, and she has guided me to build my personal finances according to my financial goals very powerfully. I am shocked to see Janvi managing finances in her twenties, so efficiently, that she can retire even in her forties with an array of streams of passive income. Even though this book particularly caters to the younger crowd, I know this book has the power to turn around everyone's perception of managing money.

Dr. Umang Gosalia
Managing Director
Parmax Pharma Limited

4. Maanav Chhetija

Finance at 21 is a great gift for every young adult! This book has proven to be a transformative resource in my life. As someone who has been working for a couple of years, I know I had previously ignored the importance of meticulous financial planning. It was Janvi who illuminated the path to financial freedom with utmost clarity. Starting this journey in my twenties has been a source of immense satisfaction, knowing I have ample time to implement the strategies outlined in the book and work towards fulfilling my financial goals with great ease. One of the most significant aspects of this book is its thorough attention to detail. The 21 tips provided in this book serve as a comprehensive road map, offering practical insights and strategies for achieving financial independence within 10–15 years. I had always heard from her, 'It's not about how much you earn, but how much you save truly matters'. Ever since this thought has gotten stuck with me and has become a guiding principle in my financial decision-making, and I'm certain that this book will do the same to you. Basically, this book is nothing short of a game-changer!

Maanav Chhetija
Network Head
Adsolut Media

5. Yash Doshi

I myself am 25, and I started planning my finances with Janvi two years ago, in 2021. Choosing to plan my personal finances with her was definitely the key to unlocking a 'Wishful' life, rather than settling for a 'Needful' one. She micromanages my finances to the extent that everything is goal-based. I am sure you can use her wisdom to manage your finances through this book, Finance at 21.

Yash Doshi
Electronics and Telecommunications Engineer

CHAPTER 1

START EARLY

TRUTH BOMB

If you are 21 and you haven't started saving yet....
you are already late by 5 years.

My father always told me that the initial years of your career are the foundation years. The way you utilize the first five years after your schooling can either make your life or leave you constantly struggling. The same principle applies to saving money. Filling your piggy bank now can prepare you for all the financial challenges that life has in store for you. However, if you postpone, delay, or ignore the principle of "starting early," you might lose a crucial part of your financial life that could have created magical years—'The Starting Years.' Despite beginning his journey of savings at the age of 11, the icon of investments, Warren Buffett, mentioned in one of his interviews that he regretted starting his savings journey late.

Having observed my father as a successful wealth coach for the past 26 years, I've had the opportunity to see people with various mindsets and lifestyles. Those who valued the principle of "starting early" have achieved commendable milestones in the area of personal finance.

Facing reality, saving money is a drag for everyone. Saving money is boring, demotivating, and not very fascinating. It might sound presumptuous coming from a 22-year-old, but yes, saving money requires a lot of effort and numerous sacrifices—sacrifices you might hate; sacrifices you might want to curse. However, with every sacrifice you make on spending, you open up an opportunity to save more.

By now, you must be wondering how you can start saving when you're just beginning your career.

I believe that each one of us can start saving from the time we learn and understand the simple meaning of the word **"SAVING."** Primary savings can begin as early as age 15 by setting aside some amount from the monthly pocket money you receive from your parents. Money received as gifts during festivals is also a great source for building and expanding your piggy bank. When you receive money from your parents to buy daily groceries for the home, resist the temptation to buy that extra chocolate or packet of chips just because you have extra money.

Out of the five hundred rupees you receive, setting aside one hundred or two hundred rupees is always an option. Unfortunately, most teenagers do not choose that option.

As you grow older, your stream of income expands through stipends received from internships and regular income generated through a job or business. The key point here is not how much you save, but "how soon you start." You can begin your savings journey with an amount as low as Rs. 500 or 1000 per month. The primary idea of saving needs to emerge at a young age so that it transforms into a habit over time.

Growing up in a family with a strong professional background in personal finance, I gained a firm grasp of this concept from the age of 18. Every income stream I developed through my summer internships, freelancing projects, and business was directed toward building my own independent piggy bank. By the age of 20, I became so fascinated with this concept that I now ensure a fixed percentage of 30 or even more of my regular monthly income is set aside for saving. I've also strived to find other avenues to increase my income so that I can expand my piggy bank during my initial years.

The importance of not just saving money but also managing it became deeply ingrained in me when I encountered real-life case studies of people who had built great fortunes, reached the pinnacle, surpassed every challenge, and amassed wealth, yet are struggling for survival today. There are countless stories of riches to rags that shook me and made me wonder how these wealthy individuals fell into the pitfall of debt. That's when I realized how crucial it is to "save when you can, not when you are forced to."

When you initially begin your career, your financial responsibilities are relatively negligible since you are yet to have a family of your own. Apart from contributing a small portion of your income at home, there's hardly any significant financial burden that you face. While it varies from person to person, the ability and potential to save are generally much higher for a younger individual than for someone in their mid-30s, who has increased financial responsibilities. Despite the age difference, I've heard many of my friends and colleagues complain about never having any money left to save.

To completely overcome this challenge and stop using "no money left to save" as an excuse, I personally started using a very simple technique for the past two years. On the first of every month—the day my income gets credited into my account—I choose saving over spending. An automatic debit into my piggy bank is scheduled for the first of every month.

By saving first, you eliminate the problem of not having enough money to save at the end of the month. Through this technique, you can spend what's left, and you're certain to be on the right path toward creating financial freedom for the future. There's no shortcut to this. Many people have an aversion to the idea of saving first and spending later. These are inevitably the individuals who believe in the fantasy of doubling their money overnight and end up with empty and torn pockets in the future.

"Starting early" has a lot to do with the power of compounding, and Albert Einstein expressed this through a wonderful statement: **"Compound interest is the eighth wonder of the world. He who understands it, earns it; he who doesn't, pays it."**

Let's simplify this with the help of an example:

Imagine two friends who grew up together. Having spent their entire childhood as friends, they decide to take up jobs at the same company. Each earns around Rs. 30,000 a month at the age of 20. During their first month at the company, they set a common financial goal of accumulating a corpus of Rs. 2.5 crores by the end of 30 years.

Friend number 1—Riya—gets very excited with her first-ever paycheck and increases her monthly expenses to Rs. 25,000. Left with just Rs. 5,000, she decides to save this amount on a monthly basis for a span of 10 years. For the next 10 years, she increases her monthly saving to Rs. 15,000 and then further increases her savings to Rs. 50,000 for the last 10 years. (5,000*12*10 + 15,000*12*10 + 50,000*12*10). Her total investment at the end of 30 years amounts to Rs. 84 lakhs.

On the other hand, friend number 2—Priya—is very calculative and decides to save a higher amount of Rs. 16,000 per month, but only for the initial 13 years, with no further saving for the next 17 years. (16,000*12*13). Her total investment at the end of this period sums up to Rs. 24.96 lakhs.

Considering an average portfolio return of 10% per annum, who do you think reached the goal of Rs. 2.5 crores after 30 years? Fascinatingly, both of them did!

If you look closely, the power of compounding worked brilliantly for Priya because she chose to save a higher amount than Riya in the initial 13 years of her career. Investing more in the initial years can relieve you from the burden of having to invest more in the future. The best part about compounding is that it's predictable and can be tailored to fit your financial ability and willingness. This is the simplest strategy for making the most of the money you earn at an early age.

Isn't this an eye-opening example for you? Just like in this example, I have decided to build a portfolio of Rs. 100 crores during my working years.

On the flip side of this rule, when you commit to start saving at an early age, you'll encounter people who will mock you for taking life so seriously, so soon. Phrases like "Take it easy," "Aren't you too young to save?" and "Enjoy your life now, savings will happen later," will be heard frequently. I have personally experienced similar situations and made the decision not to be swayed. I remained steadfast because I understood the magic of compounding in its truest sense. At times, predicting your monthly expenses may be difficult; in such cases, the principle of "save first, spend later" can be your way out. You'll also be bombarded with tempting offers to replace your wardrobe with the latest branded collection or buy the newest gadgets. But the choices you make today will shape your personal financial life forever.

Each one of us is a product of the choices we make, so why not choose wisely?

The best way to control your spending temptations and the urge to be influenced by your friends and family can be minimized by using the simple formula: Income - Savings = Expenses. This approach has helped me tremendously, and I'm sure it will help you too!

Applying this formula will take you a long way. The next chapter will explain how being conservative can still add value to this principle.

Remember, there is no "super power," "magic formula," or "secret mantra" for building sustainable wealth overnight. Be wary of people who lure you into imagining quick-fix schemes like 'double your money in 3 months' or 'multiply your wealth by 3X with us.' There are no shortcuts to creating sustainable wealth.

Key takeaways to remember:

- More than 'how much' you save, it's important to start from somewhere.

- 'Starting early' can help you gain the benefit of the "power of compounding."

- The method of 'save first, spend later' can minimize your challenge of not being able to save at all.

- And finally, there are no shortcuts to building sustainable wealth.

Note down the following:

1. What is your monthly income?

2. Mention your source of income

3. What percentage of your income are you planning to save starting today?

CHAPTER 2
BE CONSERVATIVE

<table>
<tr><td align="center">TRUTH BOMB

Anyone who spends all of their first income on extreme partying, extravagant shopping, and expensive gadgets has already started their financial journey on the wrong foot.</td></tr>
</table>

Starting your savings journey early in life is definitely a head start and will ensure smooth sailing toward financial independence sooner in your life.

A common misconception among people who have just begun their careers is the tendency to excessively accelerate their expenses due to the newfound sense of financial power. With the initial influx of income, we often develop a strong sense of authority, freedom, and empowerment. We start to believe that we own our income to such an extent that we have the liberty to spend it however we wish. Along with this newfound income, many of us think that acquiring fancy personal assets or spending lavishly on mega sales and parties will increase our value within our social circles.

I'm not promoting the idea of being stingy with money. Rather, I'm suggesting that you be careful with both your money and your expenses. When you see people around you misspending money to create a 'must-have' lifestyle, there's a high likelihood that you might be tempted to do the same for yourself. In doing so, you create a situation where you spend, spend, spend, and nothing is left for you to save. While this may seem cool at first, you're essentially digging a financial hole for yourself to fall into later.

However, adopting a conservative approach requires conscious and deliberate effort. If you're truly serious about achieving financial freedom, I have four foolproof methods that can help you become more conservative with your money.

1. Record Your Expenses

    When you take note of your daily expenses, it's important to include even the smallest ones. Within approximately 15 days, you'll gain a keen awareness of your lifestyle. This will assist you in consciously eliminating the 'not-so-necessary' incidentals.

2. Create a Distinction Between Your Needs and Wants

> We often confuse the two and end up paying for both because we lack the ability to properly identify them. Prioritize paying for your needs first, and you can allocate funds for your wants either by proactively setting money aside or using any excess funds you may have.

3. Avoid Using Credit Cards

> Credit cards can tempt you to overspend on unnecessary items, and losing track of these expenses could lead to significant debt.

4. Create Your Monthly Budget

> Based on your current monthly expenses, compile a list of essential expenditures and allocate specific amounts to each. Sticking to this budget diligently is crucial for effective financial management.

While you are on this progressive journey, it is important for you to avoid the "instant gratification" trap. This is the most dangerous trap you could fall into. It is quite common to feel the urge to indulge your never-ending demands when you receive your paycheck every month. It is also very normal to react impulsively and cater to your wants immediately due to your eagerness to practice instant gratification. The four methods mentioned above will protect you from falling into this trap.

I have never been able to find peace with two extremely opposite case studies, so I believe that finding an "in-between" could be the key to contentment. It all boils down to accepting the harsh truth that overextending yourself today could lead to a lifestyle or situation that you'll regret tomorrow. To reinforce this idea, always remember what Warren Buffett once said: **"If you buy things you do not need, soon you will have to sell things you need."**

When I started to micromanage my own personal finances and took an interest in how others managed theirs, I came across amusing yet real stories. I observed a familiar trend among many individuals: On the first of every month when they receive their income, they have plenty of money. However, that lasts for no more than 15-20 days. They then begin to struggle with their month-end expenses, live a "paycheck-to-paycheck" life, and manage their expenses through credit cards and loans. This cycle keeps repeating month after month, and they eventually form a habit of struggling with money every month. Does this happen to you as well?

Speaking of taking pride in their income and achievements, many renowned athletes, celebrities, and businessmen have lost their money while focusing on building a lavish lifestyle. Most of them have declared bankruptcy and stated that they did not have enough money to fund their survival. One of the most common case studies you may be familiar with is that of renowned tennis player Boris Becker.

He was so devoted to the sport that he was considered successful from the start of his career, having achieved six major singles titles by the age of 17. Despite the fame, recognition, and a net worth of Rs. 1,400 crores, Boris Becker accumulated a set of liabilities for himself and remains heavily in debt even today. Up until 2017, he was at the peak of his career, but since then, he has been selling off his personal souvenirs to survive and repay his debt of Rs. 617 crores. What really went wrong here?

In contrast, the life of Indian billionaire businessman N.R. Narayana Murthy tells a different story. Despite, or perhaps because of, his down-to-earth qualities and simple lifestyle, he has built a world-renowned megalithic corporation—Infosys. Today, people know him and look up to him for his simplicity. Not only has he created a very modest way of living with minimal expenses, but he also lives a respectable and peaceful life.

What we need to note here is that there are affluent people who live a simple life, and then there are those who, despite their abundance, create financial misery for themselves.

If you don't start early, becoming conservative later in life becomes difficult. Once you build the habit of tracking your expenses, you begin to think twice every time you're about to incur an expense. People around you may often confuse your conservative approach with stinginess, and continually opposing that perception can become exhausting and demanding.

What can actually help you in this situation is to complete a template of your fixed monthly expenses and track it on a regular basis. This will not only help you minimize your overspending but also give structure to your pre-decided expenses. You may want to use Benjamin Franklin's T-chart method for analyzing advantages, disadvantages, strengths, and weaknesses to make calculated decisions.

To sum it up, it all comes down to your sensitivity to how your family, friends, and colleagues perceive you. If you are affected by them thinking that you are stingy, then the battle is lost.

Remember, being conservative does not mean being stingy or laid-back. It simply means setting money aside for the multiple opportunities that will arise, opportunities that have the power to significantly improve your personal and professional financial life. This can make things better for the very same family who opposed your thought process in the first place.

Anyway, when you continually strive to be conservative, don't get discouraged if it takes time to adjust to that mindset. Breaking a paradigm that has been conditioned for years can sometimes be frustrating.

Although there is a brighter side to it. As you climb the ladder of gradually becoming conservative, you are simultaneously preparing yourself for any and every financial emergency that could come your way. In the process of building this attitude, you begin to create your emergency fund, and believe me, a lot of worries disappear when you are financially prepared to handle the unexpected. Being conservative can greatly aid you in attaining peace of mind, stability, and financial security. Once you achieve these three parameters, your focus will no longer be solely on earning money. Your primary focus will shift to much bigger and better opportunities, for which money will simply be a by-product.

Being conservative will give you peace of mind, and consistency in saving will ensure sustained financial independence for the future. In the next chapter, let's explore how consistency will add value to your financial journey and help you leverage the power of compounding in the future.

Key takeaways to remember:

- Be careful with your spending.

- Do not fall into the trap of "Instant Gratification."

- Monitor your expenses carefully.

- Ask yourself, "Where is my money going every month?"

The template provided below will help you monitor your fixed expenses and, in turn, make it easier for you to become conservative.

Sr No.	Expense	Current Monthly Amount
1	Mobile Bills	
2	Travel or Commute	
3	Contribution to the family kitty	
4	Food	
5	Wardrobe	
6	Further Education	
7	Student loan	
8	Health, Fitness and Medical	
9	Incidentals (birthday gifts to the loved ones, movies)	
10	Shopping	
11	Parties	
12	Trips with Friends	
	TOTAL	

By filling out this template, you can identify the expenses that are not so important and can be postponed. By doing so, you will consciously and deliberately have more money to save every month.

CHAPTER 3

BE CONSISTENT - SAVINGS SHOULDN'T BE A HABIT, IT NEEDS TO BE A DISCIPLINE

TRUTH BOMB

Having a well-built body two years from now requires you to do 100 crunches, 100 sit-ups, and 100 lunges today, tomorrow, and every day. The same principle applies to savings.

From having a well-built body and a successful business to maintaining a strong financial portfolio and a healthy relationship with your partner, all of these have one thing in common: "consistent efforts will make it grow." The moment you stop what you were doing to maintain the momentum, you begin to take a U-turn.

We've already seen how being conservative can simplify your life. It teaches us to differentiate between needs and wants, and it instills in us the simple rule of not overspending. Creating a budget and setting a spending limit for each month can be easily accomplished by following the template provided in the last chapter.

Any new behavior you wish to incorporate into your life must be focused on building it into a habit. Whether it's exercising regularly, maintaining a gratitude journal, or saving money, all require a strict discipline of following them regularly to achieve the ultimate result, whether that's losing weight, getting fit, or building a substantial corpus to become wealthy. The moment you take shortcuts in any of these endeavors, achieving the desired result becomes challenging.

"The habit of saving is itself an education; it fosters every virtue, teaches self-denial, cultivates a sense of order, trains for forethought, and so broadens the mind."

– T.T. Munger

Every time I meet a person, I ask them, "How much do you save each month?" The most common answer I get is, "Well, it depends on what I'm left with after paying all my bills and taking care of other expenses." This might be the case with you as well because I observe the same with the people around me. Although they are willing to establish consistency in their saving habits, they are unable to do so because they fund their extravagant lifestyles first and then save from whatever is left, if there's anything left at all.

Leadership guru John Maxwell once said, **"Small disciplines, repeated with consistency every day, lead to great achievements gained slowly over time."**

By the end of this chapter, I want you to thoroughly understand that the only path to building a money tree is through the continuous, mundane, boring, unsexy, unexciting, and challenging habit of saving money consistently. The key here is consistency.

To help you establish a consistent saving habit, I'm going to provide you with a solution that is unrelated to your monthly expenses and debts. The simplest yet effective formula for consistent saving has a threefold approach:

1. Pay your future first:

    Paying your future first essentially means saving before anything else. This could be achieved through automatic deductions, ensuring that you are steadily progressing toward your financial goals, both short-term and long-term. Aim to save at least 30 percent of your income using this approach.

2. Fund your basic expenses:

    Allocate no more than 60 percent of your income to cover your basic expenses. These encompass items such as groceries, fuel, mobile and electricity bills, loan EMIs, and so forth.

3. Fund your lifestyle expenses:

    Once you've addressed the first two categories, allocate 10 percent of your income to indulge in lifestyle expenses and treats for yourself.

When applying this formula, maintaining consistency will become much easier. I've observed many people around me adopt this approach and stop complaining about not having money left to save.

Take a deep breath, because you can do this too. You just need to make a simple shift in your mindset by starting small. The primary goal here is to ensure that you are paying your future first, whether it's Rs. 1000 or Rs. 10,000, Rs. 1 lakh or 10 lakhs a month. The amount can be gradually increased later. For now, all you need to do is adopt this approach and start saving first, making your savings consistent and non-negotiable.

Whether it's in any area of your life, consistency can lead to incremental improvements over time. A few years back, when I was closely studying the careers of successful businessmen and athletes, I noticed a common trend among all of them. Each one had a similar dream of achieving great success in life, and I'm sure you share that same dream. What sets them apart from others is their strict adherence to the rule of consistency.

On a scale of 1-10, what is your willingness to apply the simple hack of consistently repeating the smallest action over a long period of time to achieve success? Many times, you might have postponed a small action that you could have taken on a particular day, promising yourself that you would do it the next day. After all, it is a very 'small action.' You begin to use the same logical reasoning the next day and skip the smallest action once again, and the cycle continues. Very soon, instead of instilling the habit of consistency, you find yourself in a place where you are only following inconsistency. **Inconsistency can become as much of a habit as consistency, and both can be consciously developed!**

According to Charles Duhigg, the author of 'The Power Of Habit,' habits are a significant force that our brains cling to because they create neurological cravings. A behavior is rewarded by the release of pleasure chemicals in the brain. These small yet easy steps will assist you in developing the habit of saving money and making it stick.

"I accumulated small but consistent habits that ultimately led to results that were unimaginable when I started."

– James Clear.

To illustrate the true power of consistency, let me take you through a real-life case study of Oseola McCarthy (source – Wikipedia) – a local washerwoman in Hattiesburg, Mississippi. With a meager daily income of $20, she covered her expenses with $10 while consistently saving the remaining $10 each day. Without faltering, McCarthy continued to save $10 regularly, never withdrawing money from her bank account. She was content with the idea of living a simple life on just $10 per day and never felt the need to check her bank balance.

On her retirement day, she visited the bank to check her savings, and can you imagine, with her modest approach to life and powerful self-control, she had amassed a total of $280,000. Surprisingly, McCarthy chose to donate most of her savings to establish a foundation supporting education for underprivileged children. Her unwavering consistency in saving $10 per day throughout her entire journey as a washerwoman astounded the people around her.

McCarthy also wisely remarked, "It's not the ones who make the big money, but the ones who know how to save who get ahead. You have to leave it alone long enough for it to increase."

Similarly, don't worry about not having enough money to save. **Begin by saving whatever amount you can, but do so consistently.**

If you expect consistency from others in different aspects of your life, then the same principle applies to you as well. For instance, why do you expect people to be consistent in reporting, making 20 prospect calls a day, or walking 10 kilometers every day? You already know deep down that consistency is the key to success. So, be fair and hold yourself to the same standard, my friend!

I understand that it might sound challenging, but trust me, it is exceptionally rewarding. Whenever you feel derailed, think of Oseola McCarthy and how she managed to accumulate an unimaginable corpus despite being a washerwoman. Consistency helps create momentum and allows you to break down your larger goals into smaller tasks that suddenly become achievable.

Imagine aiming to build a corpus of Rs. 3 crores in 30 years. It might seem unrealistic at the moment, but by starting with a monthly savings of Rs. 14,000 for ten years, you can indeed achieve that goal. It sounds almost magical, doesn't it?

Developing consistency can indeed go against human nature, and I understand that maintaining consistent savings can be a challenging task. Randomly deciding one day to become consistent, not only in savings but also in other aspects of life, can indeed cause discomfort, raise questions, and create obstacles in achieving your ultimate goal. During your journey of saving consistently, you might encounter moments when you feel like quitting due to a lack of immediate results. This often occurs when you focus too much on the desired outcome of seeing significant growth in your savings rather than enjoying the process. This excessive focus on the outcome can lead to a loss of focus and consistency. At such times, you may feel suffocated and tempted to give up.

You must understand that nothing happens suddenly. Even when you feel pulled in multiple directions, never use it as an excuse for inconsistency. The key to avoiding excuses is immediate execution. Developing the habit of consistent saving also promotes careful spending. While this aspect is sometimes overlooked, how you consistently spend your money plays a crucial role. The beauty of consistency is that the longer you practice it, the more automatic and natural it becomes. Therefore, it's essential to build good money habits that not only involve saving money but also encompass how you spend your money.

Let's face it, if you're not consistently saving money, then it's evident that you are consistently spending it.

In the next part of this book, let's discuss "how NOT to save randomly." Making planned savings with your life goals in mind will undoubtedly help you hit the bullseye.

Key takeaways to remember:

- A continuous and consistent effort to save money for 10-15 years will help you build your financial wealth.

- There is no restriction on the amount you decide to save; what's crucial is consistency.

- Consistency is closely tied to your mental determination to achieve financial freedom.

- Swift execution of the threefold savings strategy can assist you in becoming consistent.

- The more you spend, the less consistent you become with your savings.

It's time for you to take action now!

Monthly savings	Year 1	Year 2	Year 3	Year 4
January				
February				
March				
April				
May				
June				
July				
August				
September				
October				
November				
December				
Total				
Compounded amount				

CHAPTER 4
DON'T SAVE RANDOMLY

TRUTH BOMB

CAPTCHA is random. Your savings are NOT. Ensure that your savings portfolio reflects balance, science, calculated risk, and your intelligence.

As we discussed earlier, being consistent with your savings will undoubtedly help you achieve your goals. However, saving without clear goals and a plan in place can easily derail your savings journey.

Despite understanding the importance of attaching goals to each investment, many individuals start investing randomly. They often attempt to outperform the market instead of striving to achieve their goals within their desired time horizon. Some might think, "How does it even matter if I have a plan in mind or not? I'm saving... random savings are also savings after all." Some people save just for the sake of it, invest in the market for fun, and aim to make a few extra bucks alongside their primary income source. While it's perfectly fine to start like that, continuing the same pattern indefinitely can lose meaning over time. As time passes, it's essential to structure your savings and align them systematically with your goals.

I completely resonate with an Israeli psychologist who stated, "There's a lot of randomness in the decisions that people make." This is true not only for savings but also for other significant aspects of life, such as career, relationships, and more.

Consider a hypothetical situation in which you are saving money for your higher education. It might seem vague, unclear, and indistinct until you specify that you will need Rs. 50 lakhs three years from now to complete your Masters in Marketing from the University of California, Berkeley. This clear financial goal will enable you to transform your future financial plans into definite milestones that you can begin saving and investing towards starting now.

Many athletes keep their heads down before the start of a race. But you'll notice that the moment they fix their gaze on the finishing line, they inevitably run faster. Similarly, in your mid-twenties, when you create a buzz around saving money, your focus is often directed downward to track the trajectory of your personal financial journey, with little reason to look up. However, when you treat your personal goals as the finishing line, you'll make a surprising discovery. You'll become more attentive to the milestones you achieve, and you'll be better equipped to assess whether you have sufficient time or need to accelerate your efforts.

The conclusion you must draw here is that ***"your purpose will determine your speed."***

I've heard this quote multiple times from my father, and at the age of 20, I made a firm decision that I don't want to keep struggling to earn money throughout my life. The only way to find peace with making money was to build my money tree, and that's precisely where my efforts are directed today.

What are you saving for? Are you clear about your primary purpose for saving?

If you're feeling confused and uncertain about how to transition from random investments to having a clear purpose, you might find my story interesting.

Being raised in a family experienced in managing personal finances for over two decades, I grasped the importance of saving at an early age. However, two years ago, I realized that my personal savings were not entirely aligned with my goals. It wasn't because I didn't understand the power of connecting goals to investments, but rather due to my lack of clarity in defining my goals. As soon as I wrote down my personal goals, I began to invest accordingly. My primary personal goal at the moment is to achieve financial freedom by the age of 35. I am working towards this goal by building, planting, and nurturing my two-year-old money tree. In 13 years, it will not only cover my basic and lifestyle expenses but also provide financial independence.

"If you don't find a way to make money while you sleep, you will work until you die." – Warren Buffett.

If you continue to save randomly, there will come a time when you'll realize that your finances don't bring you happiness. When you save money with a clear goal in mind, the energy, motivation, and joy of achieving milestones are multiplied. Money then takes on existential value, and your sacrifices feel worthwhile. Having a goal for which you are saving, whether for yourself or your loved ones, will channelize your efforts and inspire you to create more.

Remember, Money without Purpose, is simply paper.

Let's explore three factors to consider while saving money:

1. Short-term goals:

   Keep in mind the goals you wish to achieve within 1-2 years. These could include funding your further education, contributing to a family member's wedding, and so on.

2. Long-term goals:

   Allocate a portion of your savings for long-term goals. This could involve buying a house, a car, starting your entrepreneurial journey, or achieving financial independence.

3. Goals of your family and loved ones:

   Fulfilling the wishes of your loved ones can be a powerful motivator for saving money. It's a good idea to discuss their dreams and aspirations, such as contributing to your sister's marriage, sponsoring your brother's education, or arranging a foreign trip for your parents.

While investing heavily in fixed or recurring deposits may seem safe, putting all your money into mutual funds may appear trendy but risky. Having insurance provides security, but it often involves a long-term commitment. Simply saving based on a friend's suggestion or investing a significant sum in a single asset class may not provide the best results in the long run. Diversification and a balanced approach to investment and savings are key.

I've observed my friends' fascination with higher returns, and the stock market is their preferred asset class for investment. However, making investments without careful consideration can be risky. These investments may appear attractive initially, but it is recommended to construct a financial portfolio that reflects balance, a scientific approach, calculated risk, and your intelligence. As you assess your current savings, ensure that you have diversified your investments rather than putting all your money into just one or two assets.

I've observed my father's deep dive into understanding his clients' dreams, goals, and fears, then tailoring solutions for them using advanced financial techniques. The key here is to blend your intelligence, mindset, and intuition with contemporary financial theories when selecting the asset class that aligns with your objectives.

The financial market abounds with a variety of products, which can potentially bewilder you as you contemplate investments. This assortment encompasses bank fixed deposits, gold investments, RBI's taxable bonds, mutual funds, direct equity, real estate, and non-taxable annuities. Nevertheless, adhering to scientific principles and fundamental guidelines will aid you in crafting a well-structured financial portfolio. Therefore, rather than saving solely due to peer influence, cultivate a resolute intention behind your financial decisions.

While discovering the purpose behind saving money, you will encounter certain insights. It's important to recognize that not all your savings will yield the desired results or meet your expectations. You might be disheartened by how your savings are influenced by fluctuating market trends and economic shifts. A wise approach is to allocate your savings to portfolios that align with your goals as closely as possible. For instance, short-term goals may entail saving in a high-risk portfolio, while long-term and emergency funds may require a stable or low-risk asset class.

The distinction between saving money and investing lies in their respective purposes. Saving is geared towards accomplishing short-term goals and handling emergencies, whereas investing involves constructing a financial portfolio with the anticipation of having your money generate returns. Grasping this distinction can have a profound influence on your approach to both saving and investing.

Finally, here's an important tip: Determining your "LIFE GOALS" while saving is crucial for attaining the desired financial independence. We'll delve into this further in our next chapter.

Key takeaways from this chapter are as follows:

- Randomly saving without a plan can impede your progress in achieving your financial goals.

- Opt for informed savings in addition to maintaining a consistent savings routine.

- The more clearly defined your savings purpose, the more effective your investment outcomes will be.

- While the market offers numerous financial products, it's crucial to select products while considering the three factors discussed in the chapter.

- In personal finance, the ultimate outcome carries greater significance than the journey itself.

To eliminate random savings and create a structured approach to saving money, consider the following factors, which align with the three factors mentioned in the chapter:

	Short-term Goal	**Long-term Goal**	**Emergency Fund**
Me			
Family Member 1			
Family Member 2			
Family Member 3			
Family Member 4			
Total amount needed			

CHAPTER 5
DECIDE YOUR LIFE GOALS

TRUTH BOMB

Don't allow others to dictate who you can become and
what you can achieve. You determine whether your goal
is to emulate the next Amitabh Bachchan or the next Bill Gates.
Your savings MUST align with your personal aspirations,
not what others prescribe for you.

Now that we understand the significance of attaching goals to each investment, let's explore how we can determine our Life Goals. The process of deciding Life Goals plays a CRUCIAL role in prioritizing savings and staying focused on what truly matters in life.

If you find yourself in your mid-twenties without a clear sense of your life goals, it's essential to take stock of your direction. Are you inadvertently aiding someone else in their quest for industry recognition or assisting a millionaire in pursuing their next major endeavor? How long do you plan to support them in realizing their dreams? It's time to pause, Boss! If your vision remains unclear, there are individuals out there who will harness your untapped expertise for their own benefit, achieving remarkable outcomes in the process.

If you lack clarity in pursuing your own goals, you may inadvertently be contributing to someone else's success in achieving theirs.

You should indeed set ambitious life goals for yourself and persist until you attain them. Life goals encompass not only financial aspirations but also every facet of your life, from cultivating vibrant relationships to establishing a multimillion-dollar business and enjoying a serene and harmonious personal life.

I recently reconnected with someone I had known since childhood. We had grown up together, and I had always admired her for her dedication and commitment to every task she undertook. Her penchant for perfection and her ability to meet deadlines consistently had opened up numerous opportunities for her. I had even witnessed her seizing multiple chances for success. However, after high school, we lost touch.

A few years later, I encountered her at a coffee shop engaged in conversation with someone. From a distance, it appeared as though she was conducting a job interview. A few minutes later, I approached her table and struck up a brief conversation. During our talk, she mentioned that she was currently working as an HR executive at a Digital Marketing agency, earning a monthly salary of Rs. 25 thousand. I was surprised to hear this.

I never expected that she would settle for such a modest position. I distinctly recall her stating that she had never been too eager to start her own HR firm due to a lack of confidence, so she opted to work full-time as an HR executive with a digital marketing agency. What I realized was that her shortfall was not in confidence but in vision. The absence of clear life goals had led her to accept a life that was far below her true potential.

I attribute my ability to define my life goals to the mind power training I participated in when I was in the eighth grade. Although I was too young at the time to fully grasp the complexities of life and articulate my aspirations, I was exposed to real-life examples of individuals who had undergone the same training, applied the principles of visualization, and were now living the lives they had envisioned a few years earlier. In my naivety, I even referred to it as magic.

Over the subsequent years, after being introduced to the movie 'The Secret,' I came to understand the potency of the 'Law of Attraction.' It was then that I diligently began the process of determining my life goals. Today, I have a clear vision of what I aim to achieve in 3, 5, 10, and 15 years from now. The key point I wish to emphasize is that if you neglect to define your life goals, you'll likely drift through life, perpetually assisting others in attaining their objectives while neglecting your own.

People who do not have a plan often end up feeling disillusioned.

Life goals encompass everything you aspire to achieve during your lifetime. What's crucial is crafting meaningful goals that leave a lasting impact not only on your life but also on those around you. These goals can range from ambitious and formidable to more personal and modest ones. You have the creative freedom to shape your life goals, but it's essential to adhere to the 'SMART' goal framework while defining them (Specific, Measurable, Achievable, Realistic, and Time-bound).

To provide a structured approach to your life goals, I'll offer you a framework. I encourage you not to hastily dismiss or skim through this exercise. Take it step by step, delve into the details, and by the time you finish this chapter, you'll have a preliminary draft of your life goals. Let's start by categorizing your life goals into key segments:

1. Physical and Health Goals:

   This category encompasses both physical and mental health objectives. It's vital to give equal importance to both, as one addresses your physical well-being, while the other focuses on inner peace, stability, and contentment.

2. Relationship Goals:

   Consider the type of interpersonal relationships you aspire to cultivate with your parents, partner, siblings, colleagues, and finances, among others.

3. Career Goals:

   If you're currently employed, strategize for your next significant promotion and contemplate whether you aim to continue in your current job or if you harbor plans of launching your own company. Conversely, if you own a business, it's crucial to establish a turnover target for the next five years and explore strategic alliances to potentially triple your company's growth.

4. Financial Goals:

   This category encompasses a spectrum of financial objectives, including spending, saving, investing goals, and determining the sum you aim to accumulate within the next decade. Don't forget to include your philanthropic goals, as they are closely tied to your financial plans.

The categories mentioned above serve as a broad framework for considering the larger aspects of life. Feel free to tailor these categories to align with your personal preferences and priorities. What truly matters is that, by the conclusion of this chapter, you have a clear vision of your life goals.

Once you've categorized your life goals, it becomes crucial to grasp the true significance of establishing these objectives. The primary purpose of defining life goals is to gauge your progress and accomplishments. With a well-defined goal in mind, even an individual working at a gas station can aspire to reach the heights of success achieved by someone like Ambani. Similarly, for those with grander ambitions, a clear vision can propel them towards becoming the next Bill Gates.

Setting goals provides you with both a long-term perspective and short-term motivation to go the extra mile in pursuit of your aspirations. Moreover, when faced with an array of choices, having well-defined goals can guide you in selecting the most advantageous and progressive path.

The skill that plays the most pivotal role in driving some individuals toward success and attracting abundance in their lives is the ability to systematically set and achieve goals. Take a closer look. If you find yourself not making the desired progress in your life despite your competence, it likely indicates that your life goals are not in proper alignment. Someone with a well-defined vision and an unwavering determination to accomplish a goal will ensure its achievement, regardless of any obstacles encountered. This is the true power of defining and pursuing life goals!

When you program your brain with your life goals, your mind sends you a signal whenever an opportunity arises. Essentially, it's consistently working to align your instincts, the opportunities you encounter, and your overarching vision. One of the most significant benefits of defining your life goals is that it helps you reduce a common challenge that affects us all - procrastination. As a result, you tend to become more focused and proactive in life. After engaging in the activity mentioned above, you'll likely discover that you become more efficient in your tasks and often find yourself self-motivated.

"All successful individuals possess a goal. Without a clear destination and a vision of their aspirations, progress becomes elusive." - Norman Vincent Peale

However, the process of setting goals can become disheartening when you either have an excess of them or too few to work on. This can lead to fatigue or the frustration of hitting a plateau. Another significant setback may arise if you neglect to include goals that bring you joy and happiness. Many of us tend to approach each goal with a sense of gravity, whether it's related to our careers or personal lives. While focusing on your career or personal goals might seem like the right path, it's essential not to overlook goals in other facets of your life, such as exploring new cities or writing a book. These kinds of goals hold immense importance for your overall happiness and well-being.

When you aim to broaden your focus on pursuing life goals that bring you genuine fulfillment, it's essential to liberate yourself from financial concerns. If you genuinely seek to achieve a combination of objectives like "healthy relationships and abundant financial resources" or "good health and a thriving business," you must prioritize your goal of building a sustainable financial foundation. Otherwise, you may find yourself caught in the dilemma of "this or that," and when forced to choose between the two, one of them is likely to suffer setbacks in the long run.

Determine your life goals, cultivate your financial stability, and lead a purposeful and tranquil life!

Last but certainly not least, thinking long-term holds equal significance. This approach undoubtedly enhances clarity and provides a broader vision for life's bigger picture. We'll delve into this topic in greater detail in the next chapter.

Key takeaways to remember:

- Construct your life goals, as failing to do so may result in living a life that serves the visions of others.

- The law of attraction plays a significant role in manifesting your dreams, as it harnesses the power of visualization.

- Life goals can be categorized into various areas, with the four mentioned in the chapter being physical and health goals, relationship goals, career goals, and financial goals.

- While life goals provide direction, focus, and efficiency, the process of defining them can be complex and repetitive.

- Consider adopting the concept of 'this and that' rather than 'this or that' when structuring your goals, allowing for a more holistic approach to achieving multiple objectives simultaneously.

Write down the life goals in the following 4 categories you intend to achieve by the end of the year.

Physical and Health Goals	**Relationship Goals**
Career Goals	**Financial Goals**

CHAPTER 6
THINK LONG-TERM

TRUTH BOMB

If you plan to sustain a lifestyle of enjoyment, avoid spending all your money on partying today.

Now that you have a clear understanding of your life, let's shift our focus to your long-term goals.

In today's evolving society with changing mindsets, especially in your mid-twenties, there's a prevalent desire for instant gratification. This inclination is reinforced repeatedly, leading young people to believe that the path to success involves upgrading their lifestyles. As soon as they receive their paychecks or see a substantial balance in their bank accounts, the temptation to splurge becomes irresistible. Among the youth, there's a common mindset that questions, "Why should one compromise their current lifestyle for a distant, more secure future?" Consequently, they choose to live in the "now" and adopt a nonchalant attitude of "jo hoga, dekha jayega" (we'll see what happens), prioritizing extravagant spending over prudent saving habits.

Is your life primarily centered around planning for the next weekend, mid-term break, or extended vacation? Or do you envision a life with greater significance and purpose beyond these short-term pleasures? Are you frequently enticed by the allure of instant gratification, or do you possess a more profound, long-term vision for your life?

It all comes down to your own thoughts and beliefs, not the opinions of society!

When you start contemplating beyond your weekend festivities, acquiring the latest mobile accessories, or enhancing your wardrobe, you push yourself to escape the confines of living a predictable and commonplace life. Concentrating solely on short-term objectives carries a significant risk of stifling, disrupting, and hindering your creative potential. By encouraging short-term thinking, you essentially train your mind to focus solely on what's immediately in front of you, preventing personal growth beyond the confines of today, tomorrow, or next week.

Conversely, long-term thinking equips you to navigate both the anticipated and unforeseen challenges that life presents. It encourages you to appreciate your current circumstances rather than constantly lamenting being confined by them. When you have contemplated future possibilities, your capacity to endure present difficulties appears more manageable. Consider the individuals in your life, whether it's your parents, your mentors, or iconic figures like Steve Jobs. What significantly contributed to their growth and success was their long-term vision and the capacity to envision far into the future.

"What do you usually do when planning your vacation? Do you first identify the location or simply set off spontaneously? Much like having a long-term vision, knowing where to go is crucial. Without a clear destination, you won't be able to adequately prepare for the journey."

So, how can you nurture a long-term thinking mindset? Here are four tips you may want to contemplate:

Here are four tips to help you cultivate a long-term thinking mindset:

1. Do not get yourself out of the game:

    When one area of your life is thriving, like your business, and you're experiencing good profits, remember that it's just one part of your life. Success in one aspect shouldn't consume all your focus, leading you to neglect personal growth, your organization, or your team members. Focusing solely on one aspect can eventually take you out of the game.

2. Consciously train your mind to think long-term:

    After considering your upcoming projects and immediate goals, don't stop there. Extend your thinking far into the future, envisioning the most significant achievements you could attain in 5, 10, 20, or even 40 years. Developing the skill of forward-thinking requires practice and intention, so dedicate a few minutes each day or week to purposefully contemplate the future.

3. Do not let your current situation rule you:

    Acknowledge that dwelling on your current circumstances, such as financial limitations or unfulfilled achievements, can block your long-term vision and limit your thoughts. It's natural to find it challenging to envision a 10X profit when you're currently growing at a rate of 2X or owning a 4 BHK flat in a high-end area when you're currently renting. Shedding these limiting beliefs frees your mind and empowers you to think long-term.

4. Accept that it takes time:

    In a world where instant gratification is sought after, recognize that all endeavors require time to grow. Whether it's nurturing your financial stability or building a multi-crore business, patience and time are essential. Learning to take gradual steps before aiming for significant leaps can help you reach great heights, provided you have the capacity for long-term thinking.

As you gradually develop the capacity for long-term thinking, it's essential to assess your daily, small-scale efforts. Long-term thinking alone won't propel you toward your goals if you lose sight of your daily tasks. Long-term thinking aids in maintaining focus, but it's equally vital to consider short-term objectives, as they provide the actionable steps necessary to make progress in the right direction.

> **"Rich people think long-term. They balance their spending on enjoyment today with investing for freedom tomorrow."**
>
> **– T. Harv Eker.**

> **"All self-help boils down to choosing long-term over short-term."**
>
> **– Naval Ravikant.**

Jeff Bezos, the founder and CEO of Amazon, is renowned for his exceptionally long-term perspective, aiming to envision a century into the future. When inquisitive individuals asked him about the reason behind this extensive thinking, he stated, "We can't realize our potential as people or as companies unless we plan for the long term." This philosophy not only inspired Amazon's shareholders to adopt a long-term mindset but also enabled the company to distinguish itself and consistently attain significant milestones year after year.

Therefore, if you're not immersing yourself in contemplating your future, you might unknowingly be stifling your true potential. A fundamental aspect of achieving success lies in the deliberate and conscious practice of long-term thinking about what lies ahead.

Cultivating the habit of long-term thinking is closely tied to effective personal finance management. Whether you're torn between enrolling in a top-notch management course or hosting an extravagant party, your long-term vision can guide you in curbing the urge to overspend needlessly. Long-term thinking encourages more purposeful decision-making, fostering exponential growth as you become increasingly mindful of the choices you make.

Interestingly, when you're young, you have more leeway to make mistakes and learn from them, thanks to the ample time you have on your side. I understand that envisioning your life at 40 or 60 can be challenging when you're in your twenties. Additionally, the idea of prioritizing long-term thinking over current spending patterns may not seem particularly appealing. However, what can assist you in overcoming these limiting thoughts is the clarity you gain after defining your life goals. Once you recognize the need to fund the inevitable events in your life, you'll begin to appreciate the significance of thinking long-term.

While the distant future may seem beyond your control, you still have the ability to influence many aspects of it, as life comprises both certain and uncertain events. By contemplating the long-term, you create an opportunity to prepare for the inevitable events that lie ahead, starting today. Life's unexpected challenges may knock you down, but if you're equipped for the bumpy ride, your chances of navigating them successfully increase significantly. While you can't predict every twist and turn in life, you can certainly proactively plan and be financially prepared for the events you know are bound to happen.

Thinking long-term isn't rocket science, nor is it a magical solution for achieving all your dreams. Instead, it acts as a mental reprogramming tool, enabling you to think ahead and prepare accordingly.

While you engage in long-term thinking, remember to take action in the short term. Simultaneously, don't neglect the importance of considering your family's goals and expectations. How to do this? We'll delve into it in the next chapter.

Key takeaways from this chapter:

- Your life extends beyond weekend plans and extended vacations; infuse it with purpose.

- Avoid becoming overly fixated on long-term thinking to the point that you neglect the small steps necessary to reach your goals.

- Strike a balance between long-term vision and short-term action.

- Forward-thinking can help you recognize and tap into your true potential.

- Embrace the four ways discussed in this chapter to break free from limiting short-term thinking and embrace a more future-oriented mindset.

Write down 5 things you would like to achieve in the next 10 years and your action plan to achieve them.

Goal	Action Plan to achieve the goal	Deadline
1		
2		
3		
4		
5		

CHAPTER 7

UNDERSTAND YOUR FAMILY'S GOALS & EXPECTATIONS

TRUTH BOMB

Blessings have a ripple effect. Make sure to keep receiving blessings from those who have sacrificed their goals to help you achieve yours by fulfilling your financial responsibilities towards them.

By now, you may have realized the importance of setting goals and long-term planning. While you comprehend all of this, it's equally crucial to remember not to overlook your family's goals and expectations.

When you were young, I'm certain you observed your mom sacrificing the last bite of your favorite food so you could enjoy it. I'm sure you witnessed your dad working beyond regular hours to provide a good life for you. I'm sure your grandparents shared stories from their past, not to emphasize their struggles and hard work, but to genuinely express happiness that you're fortunate not to endure what they did. I'm also confident that you don't take any of it for granted!

I want you to take a moment to reflect on these moments from your life. As you recall your past experiences, consider how you can fulfill your role in bringing happiness and pride to those who have sacrificed for you.

I've seen numerous individuals in my surroundings experience the positive ripple effect of receiving blessings from those who have made significant contributions to their lives. Some of you may have grown up in families where members expect your time, while others may expect financial support from you.

Have you ever taken the time to contemplate your family's goals and expectations? Even if they don't explicitly express their desires, they do have underlying expectations. If you're fortunate, your family may hope to see you succeed, grow exponentially, become independent, make ethical choices, and more. The list is extensive, but none of these expectations involve materialistic demands like buying them a lavish second home or sponsoring extravagant trips abroad. Their desires are non-materialistic. The only way to uncover their hidden expectations is by spending quality time with them and generously fulfilling even their smallest requests.

The scenario described above typically applies to well-off families with no financial constraints, where each family member is self-sufficient.

That's why they primarily seek your time as a form of repayment for all they've done for you. To honor and appreciate their support, you should adhere to the fundamental family values, spend quality time with them, and go on vacations together, among other things. However, this may appear impressive only as long as you can maintain it. If you veer away from these commitments, they can become unmet expectations. While shouldering responsibilities is admirable, living up to them is what truly counts and deserves recognition.

When I reflect on my grandparents' way of life or my parents' early struggles, I genuinely consider myself fortunate. I continue to marvel at how they managed to fulfill my countless, often unreasonable requests while expecting nothing in return from me. Even today, I am both awed and humbled by their sincere desire for my personal growth and success.

Before long, one thing became crystal clear in my mind: family is a support system you never have to purchase. Through thick and thin, they will always be there to uplift and assist you on your journey to achieve your life goals. They serve as an unseen backbone behind all your triumphs and accomplishments.

To meet your family's expectations effectively, it's crucial to first identify them clearly. Failing to do so can lead to confusion about their true desires and intentions.

While non-materialistic goals demand your time and effort, materialistic goals require financial resources. Materialistic goals often arise in families facing economic constraints. In such situations, it's essential to find ways to alleviate their financial burden as you begin to earn. Anticipate areas where you can contribute even before they voice their needs. Understanding their life stories and the numerous sacrifices they've made, I genuinely believe that each of you bears a significant responsibility to learn from their sacrifices and strive to fulfill their unfulfilled dreams.

You may have also encountered situations where you observed them set aside their own dreams in order to ensure your dreams were realized in a timely manner. In such families, the probable financial responsibilities could encompass siblings' marriages, education, parents' welfare, their medical expenses, planning for their retirement, settling their debts, and striving for self-sufficiency in covering your personal, lifestyle, and future educational expenses.

The list may continue, and it can differ from one family to another. However, the key point remains that you must live up to your family's goals and expectations, whether they are financial or non-financial. By now, you might be contemplating whether non-financial expectations are more preferable than financial goals. For some, additional financial responsibilities could be burdensome. Moreover, failing to meet any of your family's financial goals might result in unwelcome sarcasm. Being unable to support your sibling's school fees can be challenging, and missing rent, EMIs, or personal loan payments can lead to increased interest payments. Therefore, it's crucial for you to accurately identify your family's financial goals to avoid inadvertently creating complications.

Whether you reside in a nuclear or joint family, surprisingly, each family member harbors specific expectations from you.

You can effectively and peacefully meet your family's financial responsibilities if your own financial situation is well taken care of in advance. Just imagine being stuck with high rent payments, repaying your educational loan, and taking on the responsibility of funding the family's monthly expenses. Not only can this create an imbalance in your financial planning, but it can also take a toll on your mental well-being. A significant financial burden can impact both you and your family. Struggles in managing relationships at home may lead to social withdrawal, sleepless nights, anxiety, depression, and increased physical ailments such as frequent headaches and heart diseases. All of these factors can weigh you down and make you feel utterly worthless.

To ensure that you never encounter any of these issues, I urge you to start concentrating on smart, systematic, and scientific management of your personal finances. Additionally, gain a more profound and evaluative comprehension of your family's goals and expectations. However, if you've already found yourself in this predicament, your utmost priority should be to extricate yourself from it promptly.

However, there will come moments in your life when you'll find yourself torn between the diverse needs of your family members. As your family requires your support, if your intense focus on saving money remains steadfast, it may be met with disdain, frustration, and disbelief. You'll find yourself in a dilemma, balancing your monthly savings against crucial family expenditures such as medical emergencies, unexpected costs, your sibling's school fees, and even everyday essentials. In situations like these, don't burden yourself with guilt for being unable to juggle both priorities.

Take a brief break! Grant yourself some respite and release from this weight.

You can opt to prioritize your family's requirements because they rely on you. You can always return to your savings endeavor at a later point. However, when you make that decision, consider these four fundamental steps:

1. Establish a return date for reengaging with your personal finances.

2. Engage with an accountability partner who can provide an impartial perspective.

3. Communicate your intention to your family members regarding your desire to resume your personal financial journey.

4. Consult with your financial coach about your plans.

Show empathy towards your family as well, for you cannot be entirely absorbed in saving money while your family is in need.

Lastly, as you jot down your goals, align your investments with your family's needs. Keep in mind that it's crucial to link a specific goal to each of your investments. We will delve into this concept further in our next chapter.

Key takeaways from this chapter:

- Dedicate ample time to reflect on your family's sacrifices while comprehending their objectives and obligations.

- Recognize that their goals and expectations may encompass both financial and non-financial aspects.

- Achieving the financial goals and expectations of your family necessitates a crucial element: money.

- Conversely, fulfilling non-financial goals requires sincere time and effort.

- Meeting your family's expectations can lead to a ripple effect of receiving numerous blessings.

Determine which category of family goals and expectations you will or must address. Create a comprehensive list and seek validation from your family to prevent future conflicts.

Family Member	Their Goals & Expectations	Your Contribution
1		
2		
3		
4		
5		

CHAPTER 8

ATTACH A GOAL TO EACH INVESTMENT

TRUTH BOMB

Become an astrologer for your own life. Predict the expenses that you KNOW will happen. Strategize your savings so that you can reach your goals on time, every time.

Now that you have a clear understanding of your investment goals, your personal needs, and your family's expectations, it's time to commence your investment planning. Assigning a specific goal to each and every investment you make adds value and purpose to your savings and investment journey.

Through my experience in the realm of personal finance management, I've come to realize that many individuals are forced to abandon 95% of their goals, not because they face economic constraints, but due to their inability to grasp the fundamental significance of goal-oriented investments. By now, I'm confident that you've embraced the concept of the importance of savings and the critical necessity of channeling your savings strategically towards your objectives.

During my research on goal-based investments, I became deeply engrossed in understanding how they can truly work wonders for individuals.

The common scenario for many individuals, and you may find yourself in this situation as well, is the tendency to overlook aligning your financial goals with your current financial situation. This oversight often occurs because you are deeply involved in meeting your daily financial obligations, which demand constant attention. Frequently, the concept of "attaching a goal to each investment" is widespread among the masses.

In this chapter, you will acquire a clear understanding of what goal-based investments truly entail and how they can prove to be highly beneficial for you.

Despite the money you may accumulate through your hard work, are you genuinely able to achieve all your financial goals as planned, or do you rely on your family to finance them? I've observed many individuals taking out substantial loans to pursue higher education, purchase their first car, and so on. In fact, a significant portion of their luxuries is also financed through loans. They become so accustomed to financing their goals with loans that it becomes a comfort zone for them. Eventually, their primary motivation for earning money revolves around repaying the substantial debts they've incurred.

When you're in the process of selecting the key financial goals you want to plan for, it's crucial to begin by comprehending the two distinct types of goals.

1. Non-negotiable Goals

    Achieving non-negotiable goals is essential for improving your life, and not accomplishing them is not an option. Therefore, there's no room for bargaining. For example, funding your higher education, providing initial capital for your upcoming business, covering the family's monthly expenses, or repaying debts are non-negotiable. If you're responsible for your sibling's education and marriage, those also fall into the category of non-negotiable goals. You cannot afford to take risks with such goals at any point because doing so can affect your relationship with your family and the well-being of a family member.

2. 'Nice-to-Have' Goals

    These goals contribute to making your life more comfortable, convenient, and luxurious. Examples include purchasing a new house, a new car, going on an international vacation, and upgrading your wardrobe with branded clothing and high-end accessories. It's acceptable to postpone or forgo one of these goals when you're struggling to manage your finances.

Once you have differentiated between the two for yourself, remember that giving priority to 'non-negotiable goals' over 'nice-to-have goals' holds significant importance.

When you begin associating goals with your investments, you develop a mindset that each investment will eventually finance a specific future goal of yours. Over time, you will develop a perspective and a habit of thoroughly evaluating each investment before deciding to proceed with that particular asset class.

"A goal is not always meant to be reached; it often serves simply as something to aim at and focus your energies on."

– Bruce Lee

If you reflect on your past and revisit the memory lane four to five years down the line, you may realize that each goal you set had a specific timeline for attainment. For example, if you decided to pursue a Master's in Marketing, you had five years to gather the necessary funds. Similarly, if you planned to get married in three years, you had ample time to secure the finances. However, this is not often how we approach such goals. Instead, we tend to take it easy and adopt a casual attitude rather than a proactive one.

I can envision what you might have done. You might have thought that you had plenty of time and would figure out how to manage the money when the time came. In case you couldn't secure enough funds, you might have compromised on your goals. To avoid ever having to sacrifice your dreams and goals, it's essential to focus on 'goal-based investments.'

Your mind might be wondering, "Does this work for everyone?"

Attaching a goal to your investments is typically advantageous because it provides a sense of purpose to investing and assists you in selecting the appropriate investment products. Furthermore, it instills discipline in your investment approach, driven by the underlying desire to achieve your goals within the specified timeframe. When selecting asset classes, whether knowingly or unknowingly, you naturally construct a diversified financial portfolio since each goal necessitates a different asset class.

For example, if you require Rs. 12 lakhs in three years to purchase a new car, a calculated investment in mutual funds starting today can help you reach that amount. However, if your goal is to generate a fixed passive income of Rs. 2 lakhs per month after ten years, you might need to adopt a more conservative strategy, with the majority of your investments in debt funds.

However, at times, you may encounter challenges when trying to link a specific goal to your investments, especially if your goals are few in number. This situation could lead you to save your money without a clear purpose, and there's a significant chance that you might end up saving less than you could, despite having the financial capacity to do so. Having fewer goals might also steer you toward adopting a traditional investment approach, where the main focus is solely on achieving higher returns.

"Sometimes the smallest step in the right direction can end up being the biggest step of your life." Believe me, saving in the right direction can help you achieve your dreams with great ease, even if they require a substantial amount of money.

However, in reality, the situation isn't always as straightforward as one might think. If your family business is thriving, you've recently received a promotion at your job, or your startup has made significant strides, it's likely that you won't be overly concerned about arranging funds for major milestones in your life. This tendency arises because you're deeply engrossed in growing your current income, making it seem unnecessary to consider your future expenses.

Goal-based investments also encourage 'guilt-free spending.' When you are confident that you are effectively managing your financial goals, the inclination to use your remaining income for indulging in luxuries becomes a source of enjoyment. I emphasized the importance of setting long-term goals in the previous chapter to help you recognize that certain expenses are inevitable, even if you may subconsciously acknowledge them. However, documenting these expenses can provide you with the assurance that you are well-prepared.

As someone who appreciates setting challenging goals that drive me to work harder each day, I value prioritizing well-planned achievements over burdensome sacrifices. If you share the same perspective, it's time for you to take control of your personal finances by documenting your foreseeable expenses. While doing so, consider allocating a specific amount for emergency funds, which can be used to address unexpected expenses that may come your way.

"While saving money is a commendable practice, failing to attach a goal to it is immature and lacks direction." Now, let's explore how, with our goals in mind, we can begin cultivating our very own "Money Tree" to nurture the growth of our investments.

Key takeaways from this chapter:

- The absence of goal-based investments can result in compromises and sacrifices when striving to achieve your goals.

- Goal-based investing is instrumental in meeting your personal needs through a well-defined investment strategy.

- Financial goals can be categorized into two types: 'non-negotiable' and 'nice-to-have' goals.

- Attaching a goal to your investments promotes disciplined savings and planned expenses, while failing to do so can lead to impulsive decisions, inadequate investments, and delayed goal attainment.

- It's essential to plan for both predictable and unpredictable goals, ensuring you are prepared for various financial scenarios.

Complete the below table to ensure efficiency towards goal-based investments.

Goal Name	Amount required to fulfil the goal	Classify your goal: 'Non-negotiable' or 'Nice-to-have'	Which Year
1			
2			
3			
4			
5			

Once you have filled out the table, it is crucial to prioritize your financial goals to determine which one to begin planning for initially.

CHAPTER 9

BUILD YOUR OWN MONEY TREE

TRUTH BOMB

Good things take time. Be it coffee, biryani, children, love stories, or savings – the best ones need patience.

Having completed the process of setting life goals, planning investments, and comprehending your family's goals, we will now explore how to construct your very own "Money Tree."

In an era characterized by instant coffee, get-rich-quick schemes, and the quest for rapid weight loss, there's a valuable lesson to be learned from the Chinese bamboo tree. In its first year of planting and nurturing, there are no visible signs of growth or existence. The next three consecutive years also yield no apparent growth or development. However, once the fifth year arrives, something remarkable happens. Within a mere six weeks, the Chinese bamboo tree shoots up to a towering height of 80 feet.

This serves as a powerful reminder that patience carries its own rewards. The question is, are we willing to wait patiently? People who are unwilling to delay gratification often settle for smaller achievements and condition themselves to expect immediate results for every action they take, missing out on the perspective of perseverance.

The Chinese bamboo tree serves as a fitting analogy for our own journey of cultivating patience deliberately and experiencing exponential growth. If the farmer had succumbed to impatience, seeking to measure the tree's growth or replace the sapling, he would have never succeeded in nurturing a tree of such towering height. While the initial stages of substantial growth may seem sluggish, imperceptible, frustrating, and devoid of rewards, it's crucial to remain patient and persistent until you reach the ultimate year of remarkable growth.

Similar to the Chinese bamboo tree, you must plant your "money tree." It undoubtedly takes ten to fifteen years to grow, but once it reaches maturity, it stands taller and stronger than any of the surrounding trees.

A money tree entails investing money in a diversified array of financial assets over a period of ten to fifteen years, with the primary aim of constructing a financial portfolio that provides a consistent and predictable income stream. It also emphasizes the creation of multiple income streams through your portfolio, which can fund all your major financial obligations, even during challenging times. Planting a money tree demands meticulous calculations to determine the amount of income you aim to generate through it. This calculation should consider not only your financial milestones but also the level of passive income required.

You might be wondering, "Is this truly achievable? Can it also be maintained sustainably?"

Everyone envisions working tirelessly, day and night, to pursue their goals and dreams. This level of dedication is often feasible during the early years of your career when your physical energy supports you. However, what happens afterward? What occurs when your health begins to decline, and you become burdened with conditions like diabetes, hypertension, high blood pressure, cholesterol issues, back pain, and chronic acidity? How will you handle your financial obligations and monthly expenses at that stage?

Cultivating a money tree can alleviate many of these concerns, as it comes with numerous benefits. The earlier you plant your money tree, the more advantages you can reap. Some of these include:

1. Accelerates Financial Freedom:

    Many individuals who commenced cultivating their money tree in their early twenties have discovered themselves achieving financial independence in their late thirties or early forties.

2. Provides the Freedom to Work on Your Own Terms:

    When you are grappling to earn a living, you often compromise your values and find yourself collaborating with individuals or entities that don't align with your principles due to the pressing need for income. However, with your money tree firmly rooted, you become your own boss.

3. Ensures a Peaceful Life:

    Money-related stress is known to be one of the leading causes of frustration globally, and it tragically contributes to a significant number of suicides. Yet, when you possess your money tree, your life is characterized by profound serenity.

4. Fosters Healthier Relationships with Family:

    With more time available to invest in your relationships, you can channel a substantial amount of your energy into nurturing quality bonds with your loved ones, consequently fortifying your connections.

5. Allows Time to Focus on Life and Attract Bigger Opportunities:

    When financial concerns cease to dominate your thoughts, you gain the capacity to contemplate life from a broader perspective. Liberated from the constraints of fixed work hours, you can redirect your focus toward identifying opportunities that possess the potential to substantially enrich your professional life.

I know many individuals among my father's clientele who grasped the concept of the Chinese bamboo tree and planted their own money tree several years ago. Following my father's advice, they refrained from second-guessing, avoided digging up the soil during the planting process, diligently nurtured and tended to it, and displayed unwavering patience for a fifteen-year period. Today, they are reaping the tremendous benefits of owning a money tree and relishing its fruits, completely free from financial worries.

Likewise, I began cultivating my money tree at the age of 20. Now, two years into this journey, I am confident that I will attain financial independence by the time I reach 35 or 37. The prospect of retiring financially at such a young age already fills me with great excitement.

All I need to do is work for income for a mere ten to fifteen years, and then I can relish a life without any financial concerns.

While the idea of having a money tree is appealing, it's essential to consider certain aspects. As enticing as it may seem, establishing a money tree from the ground up demands genuine and sustained commitment, which you must be prepared for. Failing to uphold that commitment can potentially disrupt the desired outcomes. Therefore, you cannot withdraw from the process at any point during the fifteen-year span. Doing so may result in an imbalance between projected and actual results in the structure of your money tree. Furthermore, the entire process necessitates meticulous care and attention.

As I began to engage in frequent conversations with individuals of my age group, I consistently noticed that the concept of planting a money tree has yet to gain widespread acceptance. Many people hold the assumption that their income is perpetual and that their job or business will continue to thrive indefinitely. Particularly among those in their early twenties, there is a prevailing sentiment that starting this process so early is futile, coupled with a tendency to overlook the possibility that favorable circumstances may not persist indefinitely. A significant number of people in my age bracket are unwilling to embrace this concept willingly, citing the popular philosophy of 'you only live once.' They often argue that if they start setting aside a portion of their monthly income for savings at such an early stage, they will be deprived of the opportunity to fully enjoy life.

Despite my acknowledgment of the counter viewpoints, I still advocate for the notion of establishing a money tree right at the outset of your professional career. Excitingly, I am going to guide you through two straightforward and specific methods for nurturing your money tree:

1. Follow Solid Financial Advice from an Experienced Expert:

    Regardless of the personal finance authority you choose to follow, make an effort to absorb the scientific techniques they recommend for nurturing your money tree.

2. Maintain a Stringent Financial Discipline:

    Once you commence the process of growing your money tree, there should be no looking back. Committing to financial self-discipline will enable you to achieve your desired outcomes within a specific timeframe.

The choice of which category you wish to belong to is yours to make!

At what age do you plan to start planting your money tree?

———•———

As you're busy strategizing the growth of your money tree, remember to maintain a spirit of generosity when it comes to essential expenditures in your life. We'll delve deeper into this topic in our upcoming chapter.

Key takeaways to remember:

- Learn the art of patience from the farmer who grows the Chinese bamboo tree. It takes 10-15 years to cultivate your independent money tree, requiring constant and attentive care.

- A money tree is designed to construct a robust financial portfolio, ensuring lifelong benefits and a stress-free life.

- The earlier you plant your money tree, the more time you have to nurture it.

- Owning a money tree allows your money to work for you.

You can initiate the following exercise to begin building your money tree: Create a financial forecast for yourself for the next 15 years.

Year	Expected increase in monthly expenses at the rate of 7% inflation every year
1	
2	
3	
4	
5	
6	
7	
8	
9	
10	
11	
12	
13	
14	
15	

This table will assist you in recognizing the year-on-year rise in your monthly expenses. Consequently, you should plan for your financial freedom accordingly.

CHAPTER 10

BE GENEROUS

TRUTH BOMB

Don't skimp on essential items to kickstart your career in style – invest in a respectable wardrobe, share a small celebration with loved ones, and make a modest contribution to those less fortunate than you.

Building a money tree is important, and so is saving and investing. However, when faced with the choice between these two opportunities, it's crucial to understand the distinction between your needs and your wants. Adequately funding your needs is a necessity. However, if you allocate a significant portion of your income to your wants, you're committing a grave mistake. This mistake can lead to the harmful habit of consistently prioritizing your wants over your needs. Your needs deserve more attention in terms of financial resources, time, and effort than your desires. Neglecting your needs means forfeiting opportunities that could lead to significant personal achievements.

The primary distinction between our wants and needs lies in "self-control." Without it, we often convince ourselves that whatever we desire is something we absolutely need. However, once you master the art of self-control, you can elevate your thought process, make informed choices, and exercise sound judgment.

Once you establish this distinction, it's crucial to be open to spending money on self-improvement. Being generous with funding your needs plays a pivotal role in shaping your future experiences. When you allocate money for self-growth, you are essentially enhancing your well-being. Rather than mere spending, I prefer to call this activity 'investing.' When you invest in purchasing a book, a gym membership, healthy beverages, or protein bars, you're not simply 'spending' money; you're making an investment in the enhancement of your personal growth. Compromising on these investments is never a wise decision because it means settling for a life that is not as fulfilling and powerful as it could be.

To gauge the extent of your generosity, please select one option from each statement. Choose the option that best aligns with your daily practices:

1. Small celebrations with your loved ones versus extravagant parties.

2. A smartphone fitting your budget versus iPhone 12 Pro bought on EMI or requested from your parents.

3. Spending quality time with your friends at a coffee shop versus going to a club every weekend.

4. Using cheaper transportation for extensive and frequent travel versus taking a cab to work every day.

5. Filling your wardrobe with only high-end and branded accessories versus online shopping for heavy discounts.

Making a choice might have been challenging, but did you notice a common pattern in your thinking? Your brain is often wired to follow society's norms and lifestyle choices. If you see your friend getting a new phone, you feel the desire to have it too. When your cousin shares a Facebook story of dining at a fancy restaurant, you want to dine there the very next day. These instant gratifications provide temporary satisfaction, but why allocate a significant portion of your income for a few days of fleeting pleasure? Why invest in an extra pair of branded shoes or throw extravagant parties that your friends won't even remember after two months? If you wish to follow society's lead, why not opt for choices that will genuinely benefit you in the long run?

Take the initiative to sign up for the online course your senior recommended, allocate an additional ten percent of your income to invest in the stock your friend suggested, and consider joining the fitness program your sibling recently enrolled in. This is how you can adhere to the principle of being generous towards your needs.

Since childhood, I was fortunate to be born into a privileged family where my every demand was met with convenience. My parents took excellent care of my needs, shielding me from life's harsher realities. While I am grateful for this pampered upbringing, I also owe a debt of gratitude to my coach, Mrs. Vijaya Suvarna, the MD & CEO of Liberation Coached Pvt. Ltd., for providing me with a valuable reality check.

In the past, I had a rather carefree attitude, not giving too much thought to my career, finances, decisions, or life in general. I enjoyed a life of ease until I decided to step into the shoes of those living more ordinary lives with significant financial responsibilities. After numerous discussions with my coach, I embarked on a six-to-eight-month journey of what I call 'method-living' to truly understand the subtle distinction between my needs and wants.

Despite working in my father's company, I requested him to treat me like an ordinary employee. This meant adhering to all company rules, including accepting salary deductions for tardiness and adhering to standard working hours. Not only did I adopt this approach at work, but I also informed my family that I intended to lead a financially responsible life without relying on their support. I intentionally increased my responsibilities, managing my monthly expenses and lifestyle independently.

During this transformative journey, my primary goal was to gain experiential insight into the difference between needs and wants. It required continuous effort to resist the temptation of frivolous spending. What I discovered was not only the importance of saving money but also the equal significance of meeting basic needs.

On the flip side, it is possible to harm yourself when you are overly generous. When you start to prioritize your individual needs too much, society may question your selfishness, often confusing your generosity with selfishness. I personally encountered this situation a few months ago when I chose to forgo a shopping spree with my friends because I wanted to save money for my end-of-month expenses. I wasn't surprised by the sarcasm directed at me for my sudden desire to achieve financial independence, especially given my reputation for extravagance. They simply couldn't believe that I aimed to be financially responsible and self-reliant.

Similarly, there will be instances in your life when you'll face a dilemma in choosing between two options, and you'll have to contend with the assumptions of those around you. Frustration may also disrupt your peace of mind as you compel yourself to reduce your desires and resist the urge to indulge in extravagance. You might even find yourself tempted to divert your income towards fulfilling your wants, thinking that life is too short to solely focus on basic survival needs. However, I'm not suggesting that you should lower your living standards and lead an excessively dull and serious life. What I want to propose is that the early years of your career hold great importance. While you work to strengthen and increase your active income, it's advisable to also develop the habit of saving.

Saving money becomes achievable when you consistently prioritize spending on your needs over your wants. We all enter this world on equal footing, but the life we each lead is a result of the cumulative choices we make. The decision to be prudent in fulfilling your needs while exercising restraint in indulging your wants can propel you into an entirely different trajectory in life.

Key takeaways to remember:

- Prioritizing funding your needs during the early years of your career is more critical than developing the habit of spending on your wants.

- Self-discipline is the primary tool for managing and reducing your ongoing extravagant expenses.

- Society holds the influence to shape your behavior towards their spending patterns.

- Excessive generosity can lead to stress and frustration if you cannot firmly stick to your decisions.

- Learn when to be frugal and when to be generous because overspending on luxuries is imprudent, but refraining from spending entirely is also a misstep.

- Finally, remember, even when you have the option to purchase items in installments, refrain from buying luxuries through installment plans.

It's time to take action now!

1. Identify the essential and non-negotiable needs that require funding.

2. Create a list of five wants that you will forego spending on this month.

3. Conduct a weekly assessment of your spending habits. What are your typical expenditures?

4. Analyze whether you are allocating more funds to your needs or wants on a month-to-month basis.

5. Outline three investments you would like to make in yourself for personal growth over the next two years.

CHAPTER 11
LUXURIES MUST NOT BE BOUGHT ON EMI

TRUTH BOMB

"Heavy is the neck that wears diamonds on rent,"
which conveys the message that you shouldn't flaunt diamonds
if they aren't truly yours.

You should undoubtedly prioritize investing in yourself, but if you can't afford to purchase expensive items, you shouldn't force it. The idea of acquiring everything through installment plans has taken over the mindset of society, particularly among the youth. The desire to demonstrate your worth, value, and social standing has distorted your perspective, making you believe that you must possess everything society does.

> **"Too many people spend money they haven't earned, to buy things they don't want, to impress people they don't like"**
>
> **– Will Smith.**

The practice of flaunting one's possessions has become so widespread in society that, more often than not, individuals become deeply immersed in this activity. They are unaware that, in their excessive efforts to impress others, they inadvertently start to lose sight of their own wants and needs.

"Okay… I can spend on that DIAMOND RING, pay on EMI and own it" – this is how a compulsive buyer tends to think. I know someone in my close circle who took the trend of 'showing off' too seriously. Coming from a family with significant financial limitations, his childhood wasn't extravagant. He had grown up making sacrifices and compromises. As his business gradually started to thrive, attracting new deals, his path to success became steeper. He began to elevate his lifestyle, acquiring substantial personal assets through loans. He believed that his monthly income would easily cover the hefty EMIs every month, without realizing that his monthly EMI payments soon surpassed his essential expenses. Ignorant of the fact that his EMIs were spiraling out of control, he found himself in a situation where 80% of his monthly income was consumed by these EMIs. It became increasingly difficult for him to think about anything other than paying off these loans, shifting his purpose from living life on his terms to simply servicing his EMIs.

When you become ensnared in the burden of paying EMIs, your life's focus takes a shift. Instead of relishing your work and life, you start fretting about how you'll manage to pay this month's EMI. I refer to this as 'The EMI Trap.' It's important to understand the potential consequences when you find yourself caught in this trap.

1. Although EMI schemes enable you to acquire luxuries that might have otherwise been out of reach, you're essentially purchasing depreciating assets. Over time, you end up shelling out much more than their resale market value because these assets depreciate rapidly.

2. Until you grasp just how much extra you're paying for an asset compared to its original cost, EMI schemes may seem highly appealing. While they might appear to prevent an immediate dent in your finances, it's crucial to recognize that they impose an increasing burden on your wallet over time.

3. Zero-cost EMI schemes used to captivate and entice me until I learned that there's no such thing as truly zero-cost EMIs. You've probably encountered these schemes on high-end electronic gadgets, home appliances, and other premium products. Their primary goal is to boost product sales, but believe me, there are various hidden costs associated with them.

4. In case you happen to miss even a single payment, the late fees and taxes can be substantial, making the hefty penalties difficult for you to manage.

The significant repercussions of EMI can have a profound impact on your financial well-being. If you absolutely need to borrow money for essential items, then you should do so. However, purchasing luxuries on EMI can place you under considerable financial strain.

You might be wondering how to acquire luxuries without resorting to EMI, correct? The idea of PMI (Per Month Investment) not only relieves you from the burden of loans but also greatly enhances your financial well-being. PMI involves dedicating a fixed amount of money to your savings every month, keeping it invested until you reach your goal of acquiring a luxury item. This concept isn't restricted to purchasing luxuries; it can also be applied to fund other critical financial objectives.

Let's assume that you intend to purchase a Volvo XC90 car six years from now, with a showroom price of Rs. 1,27,50,000. While many individuals might still contemplate opting for EMI, let's examine what you're potentially missing out on by not selecting PMI, using a calculation.

Using PMI to buy the car	Using EMI to buy the car
PMI – Rs. 1,25,000	Down Payment – Rs. 6,37,500
Annual Investment – Rs. 15 lakhs	Loan Taken (95%) – Rs. 1,21,12,500
Expected Return – 12% p.a.	Loan Tenure – 72 Months
Value of piggy bank after 6 years – Rs. 1.24 crores	Loan Interest Rate – 11%
	EMI – Rs. 2,30,575
Total Outgo – Rs. 90,00,000	**Total Outgo – 1,72,38,900**

Upon closer examination, you'll notice that you're essentially paying nearly double the original price. Your hard-earned money primarily goes towards making the bank wealthier. While you earn interest through the PMI approach, you end up paying interest by sticking to EMI. Similar to this example, you can calculate the amounts that will enable you to analyze 'how much extra you're paying' just for one luxury item. You'll be astonished to see how PMI can help you save a substantial amount of money instead.

Taking a proactive approach to luxury spending through well-thought-out purchases can significantly enhance your personal financial well-being. The sooner you grasp the downsides of EMI and start embracing PMI, the more likely you are to make wiser decisions in life.

If you find yourself already trapped in the cycle of EMI, here's what you should consider:

1. Repay loans with higher interest rates first:

    If you have multiple EMIs for different loans, assess which ones are costing you the most due to high interest rates. Prioritize repaying these loans first to alleviate a significant financial burden.

2. Keep EMIs at or below 30% of your income:

    Calculate how much of your monthly income goes towards paying EMIs. If this percentage exceeds 30%, you are at risk of encountering financial difficulties and an imbalanced financial life. Ideally, individuals in their early twenties who are aware of the concepts of EMI and PMI should avoid taking on loans altogether.

3. Balance Lifestyle and Essential Expenses:

    While luxuries may seem appealing, it shouldn't come at the expense of your financial peace. Begin to reduce your lifestyle expenses while you work on clearing your EMIs. By doing so, you'll have more room to cover your basic expenses as well.

I understand that it may seem challenging and demanding, but if you aspire to enjoy financial tranquility, it's imperative to extricate yourself from the growing trend of 'purchasing everything on EMI.' Especially while you're young and have time on your side, it's crucial to plan accordingly. Otherwise, you risk spending your entire life ensnared in the cycle of monthly EMIs.

Last but certainly not least, if handling everything on your own becomes overwhelmingly burdensome, consider seeking professional assistance.

Key takeaways from this chapter:

- Don't indulge in luxuries at the expense of EMIs.

- Purchasing something with a loan often results in paying significantly more.

- Differentiate between your needs and luxuries and set priorities accordingly.

- Consider creating a dedicated savings fund for your luxury purchases.

- EMI benefits the bank, while PMI benefits you in the long run.

Write down one luxury item you wish to purchase. Calculate two amounts: one if you choose PMI and another if you choose EMI. Which one would you opt for?

Using PMI	Using EMI
PMI:	Down Payment:
Annual Investment:	Loan Taken (95%):
Expected Return Per Annum:	Loan Tenure:
Value of piggy bank after __ years:	Loan Interest Rate:
	EMI:
Total Outgo:	**Total Outgo:**

CHAPTER 12
TAKE GUIDANCE FROM PROFESSIONALS

Truth Bomb

Real geniuses don't entrust their health or wealth to anyone other than experts in the field. Those who think they can manage both by themselves are definitely not geniuses.

Now that you are clear about not going overboard with your expenses, let me ask you something. Would you consult a psychologist when you are facing extreme anxiety, depression, or hypertension, or would you deal with it by yourself?

Would you go to the dentist when you are suffering from a severe toothache, or would you simply minimize the pain by taking painkillers?

Would you hire a lawyer to fight your case, or would you study the matter and represent yourself?

When you believe in taking professional help for all the above scenarios, why not for managing your personal finances? If managing personal finance were that easy, there would be no money worries at all. People wouldn't be struggling to manage their expenses, loans, savings, and other financial matters.

You might be thinking, "Investing and saving is a cakewalk. I can do it all by myself. Why should I hire a professional?"

The mindset of seeking professional help from experts is rare. What is more common among the youth is to follow what their friends are investing in, accept what is working for others, and blindly follow that. They often don't realize that by following the crowd, they could get into critical financial troubles that could lead to a financial mess.

Behind every successful individual is a multitude of people, among whom one of the most critical is their coach. Whether it's Bill Gates, Jeff Bezos, Richard Branson, Virat Kohli, or Sania Mirza, they all had one thing in common: a coach who guided them in reaching the pinnacle of their careers.

Do you think Sachin Tendulkar would have become the greatest batsman if he had practiced bowling in the initial years of his career? It was his coach, Ramakant Achrekar, who recognized his superior batting skills. Even today, he gives the highest credit for his success to his coach.

In the field of personal finance, it's time for you to choose whether you want to learn from your own experiences or from experts. To provide a clearer perspective on this thought, let's outline the major differences between a professional financial coach and an ordinary individual from whom you might seek advice:

1. In-depth Knowledge Versus Academic Knowledge

    While a professional continually researches and studies financial markets and money patterns, offering guidance based on wisdom, an ordinary individual might guide you based on what he or she read in the newspaper last night.

2. Real-Time Expertise Versus One-Case Experience

    A financial coach has multiple-case experiences due to a vast clientele, whereas an ordinary individual you rely on might give you advice based on his or her personal experience.

3. Delinking Emotions While Giving Advice Versus Advice Based on Emotional Connection

    Professionals do not let emotions interfere with their advice, whereas others who advise you may be speaking from their own life experiences, whether painful or otherwise.

4. Financial Thumb Rule Versus Vague Tools

    Professionals use scientifically proven methods and rules to determine your personal finances, whereas an ordinary individual might suggest a tool he or she learned online.

5. Professional Credibility Versus Personal Goodwill

    While a financial expert speaks with authority, authenticity, and great credibility, an ordinary individual might give advice based on what he or she has experienced and believes to be true.

"To achieve the results that only 5% of the population has, you need to do what only 5% of the population does."

– *Robin Sharma.*

While 95% of the population struggles without achieving the results they desire, the remaining 5% accomplish all the goals they have set. Which bracket do you want to fall into? If you aim to be part of the 5%, you should know that only the top 5% seek guidance from a professional financial coach to create the life of their dreams.

The fundamental reason for seeking a professional's guidance is to gain advanced clarity on where your money is actually being invested. Most of the time, people struggle to find a solid foundation for their investments, a challenge that can be minimized by considering an expert's advice. This advice encompasses where to invest, how to invest, why to invest, and when to invest.

Moreover, a financial expert can help you overcome your fear and burden of managing your personal finances. While you focus on excelling in your industry, let the expert take care of your money.

"I can't teach you your business, but I can definitely make you financially free." Do what you are best at and delegate the rest!

Taking professional help means half the battle is already won! The next important step is to choose the right portfolio.

Key Takeaways from This Chapter:

- When it comes to managing personal finance, don't follow the herd.

- Taking guidance from a financial expert means you are using scientific systems and processes to build your financial portfolio.

- The money you earn comes through hard work. Do not let your parents, friends, colleagues, or neighbors tell you what to do with it.

- All the successful people you see around you have a coach guiding them to success.

- You are the expert in your field. Don't try becoming one in the field of personal finance.

1.   What Will Stop You from Taking Help from a Financial Coach?

2.   Who Is Guiding You in the Journey of Managing Your Personal Finance?

3.   Write Down 3 Things That a Professional Financial Coach Can Streamline for You That Others Can't:

CHAPTER 13

CHOOSE THE RIGHT PORTFOLIO

Truth Bomb:

You may think owning a helicopter is cool, but if you had one today, you wouldn't know what to do with it. The same principle applies to investments: what looks awesome in general may not necessarily be awesome for you.

A professional will present you with all the possible options to choose from. You can select the best among those, aligning with your investment goals and needs, rather than randomly following what others are doing.

"Let's invest in what you think is best!"

"My friend just started a monthly SIP (Systematic Investment Plan) of Rs. 20,000, and I think I'll start that too."

"XYZ stock is being bought by a lot of people these days; should I buy it too?"

"My neighbor told me about some non-taxable plans. How amazing would it be to have tax-free investment returns!"

"Will the property market rise? Should I allocate a portion of my income to buying a unit there?"

The list is endless, but my answer to all these statements remains the same: There is no best asset class or most accurate investment option. What seems to be working well for one individual has nothing to do with it working equally well for you.

You must absorb this thought by American author Barry Ritholtz, who says, "When it comes to investing, there is no such thing as a one-size-fits-all portfolio."

There is no standard fit. Rather, financial portfolios are 'custom-fit'—tailor-made to such an extent that they can only suit you and no one else. So, the next time someone asks you to invest in equity along with them, make sure you politely decline. Analyze, evaluate, and be selfish enough to look after your own requirements when it comes to building a financial portfolio for yourself.

Speaking from personal experience, my father has adopted a conservative investment strategy to minimize risks in his portfolio, while I have directed 80% of my savings toward mutual funds. While he prefers protecting his capital at his age, my primary focus is on building a larger corpus through calculated risks. My younger age allows me to take higher risks because, in the event of an adverse outcome, I have enough time to recover any losses. In my father's case, he opts for peace and stability in his financial portfolio, for which a conservative investment strategy works best.

To begin with, it's important to understand that a series of elements need to be considered when determining what's right for you. A thorough analysis of your behavior, income, spending patterns, risk appetite, and both short and long-term financial goals should be taken into account when building your financial portfolio.

While choosing what's right for you, it's essential to understand the basic types of financial portfolios and assess their suitability for your situation. Financial portfolios can broadly be divided into three types:

1. High-Risk Portfolio

    A high-risk portfolio usually aims for growth, which involves a greater chance of losing capital or experiencing poor performance. However, it could also generate higher returns than you expect. Common financial products in this category include equities, properties, and commodities. This type of portfolio is advisable for younger people with high-risk tolerance, who are comfortable with accepting greater short-term volatility for long-term returns.

2. Conservative Portfolio

    A conservative portfolio generally consists of safe but low-yielding investments such as developed market and government bonds, cash, and property. For people who prioritize preserving their existing capital over growing it, a conservative financial portfolio works best.

3. Balanced Portfolio

> Individuals who fall between these two extremes might consider building a balanced portfolio. The initial focus here is to balance both risk and return. If you want to strike a balance between capital preservation and growth, you can invest in products like equities, emerging market bonds, and properties.

While conservative investors seek complete capital preservation strategies and aggressive investors look for growth strategies, balanced portfolios sit in the middle of the risk-reward spectrum.

One of my clients, who is in her mid-twenties, approached me with Rs. 1 lakh to invest. Considering that she has no immediate financial needs for a couple of years and intends to fund her own educational expenses for completing her PhD in medicine after five years, she could adopt a relatively risky investment strategy. Due to her youth and her current expenses being covered by her father, she has the opportunity to benefit from long-term growth. However, given her low tolerance for investing in riskier products, she opts for a conservative financial portfolio by investing in market and government bonds.

On the other hand, I encountered an individual who was open to any financial products I recommended. He wanted to ensure that Rs. 20,000 of his fixed income was saved every month after accounting for his monthly expenses, EMIs, and lifestyle costs. Being young and willing to take risks, yet responsible for his financial decisions, the asset classes had to be chosen accordingly. The Rs. 20,000 could be allocated based on his specific requirements.

Now it's important to understand that his higher education, his parents' well-being, and creating his own lifestyle are events that are bound to require a significant amount of money. These important and certain events could be planned for by investing in safe instruments that have a scientific logic behind them. Though the returns might be low, his capital will be protected. Such asset classes are typically used for long-term goals. For such important events, you should also ensure that the amount you plan on receiving in the future is guaranteed and involves minimal or no risks, because you wouldn't want to compromise on the most important events of your life.

Likewise, he could fulfill his dreams of buying a second home or taking trips abroad every year by investing in aggressive financial instruments. In these instruments, the capital is not protected but promises higher yields. He decided to adopt a balanced portfolio based on his requirements, using a 50-50 approach between equity and government bonds.

In the process of choosing the right portfolio mix, you may find yourself stuck if you fail to understand the product in which you're investing. Sometimes, if you don't see the returns you expected within the timeframe you anticipated, you might lose patience and trust in investing your hard-earned money. But don't stop investing! Don't make a U-turn. Take a moment to breathe!

Return to reviewing your financial goals and align them with your investments. Doing so will not only maintain your momentum but also help you create a diversified portfolio. If one product is underperforming, you have two other products to back you up, and that's the beauty of having a variety of products in your portfolio. Don't let your emotions get the better of you when you experience a downturn in your portfolio. Stay invested and allow the magic of holding onto your investments to work for you.

What looks good on paper doesn't necessarily translate well when you begin to implement it. While your investment strategy might appear impressive in Excel spreadsheets, actual implementation can be challenging. However, if you've identified the right mix for yourself, go ahead and begin your investment journey, as there's no better time to start!

Before you begin, make sure you're not falling into the common misconception prevalent among many individuals—that what works best and is appealing to the majority should also be part of your portfolio. Building a portfolio based on what seems trendy and attractive will not serve you well. Align your life stages with your investment choices, and that approach will likely benefit you. Also, always keep in mind that you shouldn't be influenced by your parents' investment decisions.

Key takeaways from this chapter:

- Avoid following the herd when designing your financial portfolio.

- Multiple factors such as age, income, risk appetite, and life stages need to be considered when building the right portfolio mix.

- The three main types of portfolios are high-risk, conservative, and balanced financial portfolios.

- Conservative investors aim for complete capital preservation, aggressive investors prioritize growth, and those seeking a middle ground opt for a balanced portfolio.

- There is no such thing as a 'one-size-fits-all' financial portfolio.

1. What factors will you consider when determining your portfolio type?

2. What are the key life events for which you are investing?

3. Which type of financial portfolio do you plan to create for yourself?

CHAPTER 14

DON'T FOLLOW THE FOOTSTEPS OF YOUR PARENTS

> **TRUTH BOMB**
>
> You don't dress the way your parents did.
> You don't save the way your parents did, either.
> Fashion isn't the only thing that has evolved, you know?

Now that you have selected the appropriate portfolio, it's important to review it in line with your financial and life goals.

Many of you might closely follow what your parents do, often accepting their methods as the only path to success. While there's some truth to that, it's not always the case. Just as fashion has evolved significantly, so too have saving and investing patterns. In this chapter, we will explore how financial markets have changed over time, and why it may not be advisable to invest in the same avenues your parents did.

"The true secret of success in investing money is not which asset class to choose, but rather which ones to avoid." However, your eventual choices will depend largely on how your mindset has been shaped over the years.

"Hey, my father lost a lot in the stock exchange and never saved enough because of that. I should never invest in stocks."

Your mindset regarding your personal financial journey is directly related to your parents' behavior toward money, as it plays a significant role in shaping your financial attitudes and beliefs.

If your parents declared bankruptcy in the past or lived their lives burdened with loans, you are more likely to prioritize saving money over extravagant spending. On the other hand, if you grew up in a household that values status, you may find yourself overspending to maintain your family's social standing. Similarly, if you observed your parents avoiding discussions about money or financial challenges, you might have developed a tendency to evade dealing with your own finances. In contrast, if you consistently saw your parents promote and practice the habit of saving money, you would have subconsciously adopted the habit of setting aside a portion of your earnings on a regular basis.

In some families, I've noticed that as soon as a child starts earning, parents who have always associated money with fear are quick to offer advice on how to save money. They do this because they don't want their children to lose money as they did. While there's no questioning the trust factor with parents, they may not always be the most effective source for investment advice.

On the other hand, some parents give their children the freedom to design their own investment journey. If you belong to this group, you'll find that your personal finances are much more peaceful. I know people who are entirely independent in this regard, but it's important not to confuse this freedom with disrespect. Many children think that if they don't follow what their parents did, they are disregarding them, but that's not necessarily true.

If you want to break away from your parents' approach to saving money, consider these three key points:

1. Study the Current Financial Market:

To ensure you're on the right track with your savings, check whether the asset classes you've invested in are still valuable in today's market. If not, identify which ones are currently favored and consider replacing your existing investments with those.

2. Take Charge of Your Investments:

When I offer investment advice to clients, many say they will consult their parents or relatives before making a final decision. While there's nothing wrong with seeking advice, it's important to recognize that their suggestions are likely based on their own experiences and perspectives, not on financial expertise. As a result, their advice could be biased and not necessarily useful for your specific situation.

3. Consider Professional Assistance:

If you're uncertain about your personal finances, it's often better to seek advice from a professional rather than solely relying on your parents' opinions. Professionals stay up-to-date with current financial market trends and can provide recommendations tailored to your individual needs.

As I grew up, I observed my father's admiration for the concept of saving money. Although I couldn't fully relate to it at the time, I now wholeheartedly understand. Over the years, I've seen him lead a debt-free, peaceful, yet luxurious life. Naturally, I find myself following in his footsteps, saving diligently in hopes of creating a similar lifestyle for myself.

You might be wondering about the contrast here because I previously mentioned "not to follow the footsteps of your parents." What's important to note is that you should avoid blindly replicating the exact asset classes they invested in. What worked for them during their era might not necessarily be the best fit for your financial goals and the current market conditions.

"Don't live the same day over and over again and call that a life. Life is about evolving mentally, spiritually, and emotionally."

– *Germany Kent*

let's explore this concept using two examples of how the Indian financial market has evolved in recent years:

1. Investing in property was once considered one of the most lucrative investments, with cash transactions being prevalent, and the market in a booming phase. However, the property bubble burst following demonetization. Returns became stagnant, and the property market reached saturation. If you're contemplating investing in property simply because your parents did, be aware that you may not experience the same benefits they did.

2. Similarly, investing in fixed deposits was a prevailing trend for the majority of individuals in the past. Even those with limited financial knowledge found it worthwhile to invest in bank fixed

deposits. Why? Because interest rates in the 90s were as high as 10-12%. However, as a country progresses, the repo rate tends to decline, causing fixed deposit rates to decrease as well. In those days, investing Rs. 1 lakh per month at a 10% interest rate seemed advantageous. However, if you choose to invest in fixed deposits today, you might only receive an interest rate of around 6%, and this rate has the potential to decrease further as the country continues to develop.

Investing in property is a wise choice when your goal is to acquire a second home for yourself. Saving your money in fixed deposits can also be a suitable option if you possess adequate financial knowledge and are comfortable with the gradual decline in interest rates over time. Every asset class has its own lifecycle, and it eventually reaches a point of saturation. To fully reap the benefits, it's essential to select an asset class that aligns with your current financial situation and goals.

You might encounter various objections if you abruptly cease to follow your parents' lead. Some parents insist that their children obediently adhere to their guidance and expect them to seek their counsel before making any financial decisions. If you choose to heed their advice, you should be mentally prepared that your outcomes may not mirror theirs.

If you wish to comprehend the scientific reasons behind why you shouldn't blindly follow in your parents' footsteps, take note of the three points I'm about to discuss:

1. Difference in Money Personality:

   Your parents' financial circumstances and upbringing were likely quite distinct from yours. The factors that shaped their approach to money will almost certainly differ from yours. As a result, it's unwise to adopt their spending, saving, and investing patterns. Instead, consider customizing your investment plan to align with your own money personality.

2. Evolving Times:

    Times are constantly changing. What made sense a decade ago may not be applicable or relevant to you today. This applies to various aspects of life, including fashion, technology, business trends, and financial practices such as saving and investing.

3. Different Expectations and Goals:

    Your parents probably had specific financial goals in mind when they devised their savings and investment strategies. They invested in assets that aligned with their goals at that time. If you have entirely different financial goals, it's essential to craft a distinct investment plan tailored to your own objectives and expectations.

Henceforth, listen to what your parents have to say, compare it with the factors discussed in this chapter, and make a decision that you feel will suit you best.

At the same time, it's important to realize that you should explore additional options to increase your income – all while maintaining ethical practices.

Key takeaways from this chapter:

- Your investment journey might not replicate that of your parents.

- Your mindset and financial habits can be shaped by your upbringing and past experiences.

- Choosing a different path from your parents doesn't necessarily mean disrespect; it signifies a distinct perspective.

- Beyond fashion, technology, and career decisions, our approach to saving, investing, and financial planning has evolved over time.

- You'll encounter individuals who are either heavily reliant on others or self-sufficient in their investment journeys. It's your turn to determine your group affiliation.

1.   How do you differ from your parents?

2.   What are your goals in comparison to those of your parents?

3.   In your savings journey thus far, are you mirroring your parents' choices, or are you independently making decisions? If you are emulating them, do you feel the necessity to modify your approach?

CHAPTER 15

FIND AVENUES TO EARN MORE BUT ETHICALLY

TRUTH BOMB

There is plenty of money out there, ready to come your way. It's all around you, waiting to be uncovered. And if you're savvy, you'll seize it!

Having learned from professionals and drawn life lessons from your parents, you can periodically review your financial journey.

If you aim to grow your savings, relying on a single source of income is insufficient. Given your youth, abundant energy for earning, fewer financial obligations, and the family pool or your parents taking care of most expenses, this presents the ideal opportunity to explore various avenues for increasing your savings from alternative sources.

By now, you're likely aware that it's advisable not to allocate more than 70% of your income to personal expenses, reserving the remaining 30% for savings. However, when your salary falls short, it might be necessary to utilize 80%, 90%, or even 100% of your income to cover your expenses. In such cases, you must seek additional income sources to make up for the 30% you were supposed to save. For instance, if you earn Rs. 30,000 per month and were expected to save Rs. 10,000, what if your household expenses alone surpass Rs. 30,000? In such a scenario, you must explore ways to earn more in order to set aside Rs. 10,000. The choice of assets for investment can come later, but this amount should be earmarked if you intend to effectively manage your personal finances.

By now, you're likely aware that it's advisable not to allocate more than 70% of your income to personal expenses, reserving the remaining 30% for savings. However, when your salary falls short, it might be necessary to utilize 80%, 90%, or even 100% of your income to cover your expenses. In such cases, you must seek additional income sources to make up for the 30% you were supposed to save. For instance, if you earn Rs. 30,000 per month and were expected to save Rs. 10,000, what if your household expenses alone surpass Rs. 30,000? In such a scenario, you must explore ways to earn more in order to set aside Rs. 10,000. The choice of assets for investment can come later, but this amount should be earmarked if you intend to effectively manage your personal finances.

In every organization that employs someone, there is a clause in the appointment letter that specifically states, "You will not be employed for any other commercial purpose." If this applies to you, you may need to obtain a No Objection Certificate (NOC) from your organization, which permits you to explore other employment opportunities. Essentially, this is what's known as 'moonlighting.' However, you must seek consent from your primary organization, which must approve of your additional employment to supplement your income.

There are numerous opportunities for you to boost your income without conflicting with your current organization. Examples include engaging in multi-level marketing, working part-time as a content writer, pursuing digital marketing, providing social media marketing services to close friends, or teaching part-time. Crucially, all income derived from these supplementary sources should be earmarked primarily for savings, with a small portion set aside to enhance your overall comfort and quality of life.

Besides seeking external income opportunities, you can also explore avenues to increase your earnings within your current company. In this context, it's crucial to discuss with your boss how you can supplement your income without overburdening your existing job responsibilities. Merely asking for a raise may not always yield the desired results!

Within the organization, there are various opportunities to increase your income, such as generating new clients for the company, acquiring new leads, and taking on company-offered projects. Additionally, you can participate in the employee recruitment referral program, where you introduce someone to the company and earn a reward for your efforts. Another option is selling the company's merchandise to boost your earnings. Therefore, explore different avenues within the company to expand your income sources. Most organizations are willing to reward employees for their extra contributions. This approach of diversifying income sources applies primarily to those who are employed.

For an entrepreneur, the ballgame is entirely different. Your primary source of income should originate from your own company. If you spend eight hours at your company and then work elsewhere for the next few hours, you aren't fully committed to the business you've established. It's akin to giving birth to a child and then tending to your neighbor's child. Trust me, you can't effectively manage both. Shifting between the two will prevent you from giving proper attention to your own venture. Instead, you'll likely end up feeling frustrated, agitated, annoyed, and fatigued when returning to your own company after hours spent elsewhere.

Being employed in a company typically entails 8-9 hours of work each day, while entrepreneurship is a 100% commitment, a 24/7 endeavor that demands your attention constantly as it grows. When you work for someone else, you're generally not expected to exceed 60 hours of work per week. However, with your own business, there are no set working hours. The concept of diversifying income sources primarily applies to employed individuals. As an entrepreneur, your primary income source should be your business. If you have the energy to invest elsewhere, it's often more beneficial to channel that same energy into expanding and scaling your business itself.

"Never depend on a single income. Make investments to create a second source"

– Warren Buffett

Entrepreneurs require unwavering focus. The following example will illustrate and align with my conviction.

Two years ago, I attended a conference where, at its conclusion, all participants were invited to a breakout room. Inside the breakout room were approximately ten millionaire investors, including some prominent figures in the industry, who were present to provide guidance on how to approach investors. With an audience of roughly 40-50 people, everyone had the opportunity to discuss their financial inquiries with these investors.

Among the attendees, a young man in his mid-twenties posed a question. He stated, "I work in my father's company, an electronics store that my grandfather established many years ago, and it's been quite successful. Additionally, I run my own software business and am interested in approaching an investor to secure funding for my product. My concept revolves around managing software modules for small and medium-sized enterprises. I've tested my software packages on a few businesses, and the results have been outstanding. I genuinely believe it's a valuable product and I'm seeking funding to further its development."

One of the investors on the panel inquired, "What does your typical day look like? How do you manage your schedule?" He provided a brief overview of his daily routine, stating, "I wake up at 7 am because I need to open the electronic shop at 9 am. I assist customers at the shop, complete all the day's tasks, and finish my work there by 9 pm. After having dinner and spending quality time with my family, I begin working on developing my software product at 11:30 pm. I work on it until 3 am and then get about 4 hours of sleep. Even on weekends when the shop is closed, I dedicate my time to my product. Whenever I find some free time, I invest my full dedication into it."

Upon hearing his entire schedule, the investors promptly declined, stating, "No investor would fund your software because it's not your primary business or profession; it's merely a hobby. You can't expect an investor to finance your hobby. It doesn't qualify as a profession when you're dedicating just 4 hours a day and some time on weekends to it. If you want to enjoy the benefits of your existing business, rely on your parents and family, maintain customer satisfaction in your father's business, and keep your life comfortable, all while occasionally working on your software product when you have spare time, then an investor is unlikely to provide funding. Investors expect a 24/7 commitment to the software product if they are to invest in it. If you want to pursue it as a weekend hobby, you'll have to fund it yourself."

This point resonated strongly; you can't achieve comfort by constantly juggling between your business and a hobby. You need to pick a business and commit to it. This is the key to business growth. Many entrepreneurs seek to start additional companies because they lack competence, passion, or interest in their original business. Rather than addressing these issues, they begin searching elsewhere for the same.

While those in employment have little at stake beyond their job, an entrepreneur often feels responsible for losses and the effort put into business growth, among other things. For an entrepreneur, any supplementary income source must be non-intrusive, passive in nature. It shouldn't consume your time, energy, or space, especially during the crucial early years of growing your business.

While you're young and have the energy, time, and capability to put in the required effort to increase your income, don't overlook the importance of establishing passive income sources through savings and investments, with the guidance of a financial coach. This way, if there's a break in your career, a layoff, a sudden downturn, or even if you're taking a short sabbatical to rebuild your career, your expenses can be managed effectively.

Lastly, always remember to maintain a clear separation between your personal and professional life. We will delve deeper into this concept in the upcoming chapter.

Key takeaways from this chapter:

- To increase your savings, you must have multiple sources of income.

- The theory of generating different streams of income is quite different for a person doing a job than for an entrepreneur.

- It is important to expand your income avenues but do so ethically.

- As an entrepreneur, your primary focus should be on growing your business rather than indulging in starting other businesses.

- While you are on the journey to earn more, don't forget to save for your rainy days.

After reading this chapter, I am sure you must have thought of several ways to increase your monthly earnings. Write down 3 ethical ways to increase your monthly income.

CHAPTER 16

DRAW A LINE BETWEEN YOUR PERSONAL AND PROFESSIONAL LIFE

TRUTH BOMB

Having your girlfriend at the office and your boss at home is a bad idea. The same rule applies to money.

In case you have figured out avenues to earn more, you need to know that you still have to follow the habit of savings as per the original plan. Extra income does not mean more spending.

Though money looks exactly the same, has the same color, a hundred looks like a hundred everywhere, and fifty looks like fifty everywhere, the function of each rupee is different. The money intended for building your business should only be used for that purpose. The money set aside for higher education or monthly expenses must be reserved for those specific purposes. It **cannot and should not** be mixed together.

The moment you begin to overlap one expense with another and draw comparisons between them, you start depending on each other. Just as one cannot have 'two swords in one sheath,' you cannot mix your personal and professional life. One of them has to take precedence!

What if you think, "I'm smart enough to handle both simultaneously"?

Either you will end up using the money intended for organizational growth to meet family needs, or you will exhaust all the funds earmarked for personal use in expanding your business. Mixing money for personal and professional life is not a winning strategy, especially at the outset of your career. Instead, it's a zero-sum game. If you allow them to compete against each other, one will invariably hinder the other's growth. Keeping them separate, managing them separately, nurturing them separately, and allowing them to grow independently is the only way to ensure their individual growth.

If you had two extremely headstrong daughters-in-law in the same house, it would be challenging for everyone to coexist. Hence, it's better to have them in two separate homes. Similarly, two brothers with entirely different thought processes would likely prefer not to live together. This analogy mirrors how you should handle money when managing your personal and professional life.

Most business owners tend to withdraw money from their bank accounts or company accounts to serve their extravagances. They use the company's money for parties, movies, and shopping. The company ends up funding their comfortable lifestyle while they indulge in a spending spree. I've seen many of them making personal purchases and submitting the bills to their own company for reimbursement. If you too are doing this, you are cannibalizing your own company and depleting its resources.

Any financial coach would advise you to withdraw a specific amount from your company every month. This amount can vary, but it's crucial to restrain yourself from withdrawing any more. Similarly, even government agencies adhere to a protocol of establishing budgets for various purposes, whether it's for emergencies, infrastructure development, or pipeline reconstruction. They maintain separate budgets for each requirement and are not allowed to commingle funds or shuffle them as per their needs. This separation is a fundamental principle in financial management.

Money has a tendency to erode and consume whatever you had set aside. It also ensures that if both aspects of your financial life cannot succeed simultaneously, at least one can be preserved. It's akin to sailing on the same boat; if the boat is sinking, everyone on board will sink. However, if you have two boats and people are divided, if one sinks, there is another as a backup. Similarly, when you manage your finances in two separate aspects, at least one part of your life will be secure even if the other is struggling.

"You only have to do a few things right in your life so long as you don't do too many things wrong."

– Warren Buffett

I have been working with my father for more than two years now, and he has instilled a strict discipline in our family. Each family member with their own source of income is responsible for managing their personal expenses from their own pockets and through the salary they earn. I handle everything from sponsoring my own petrol to taking care of my monthly expenses and growing my savings from the salary I receive. Similarly, if you're a business owner who relies on your company to cover your expenses, I'm sorry to say, that's not the ideal approach. Billing the company for every personal expense will create a high level of dependence on the company's income. What will you do when the company is facing losses? Will you be able to ask your family to go hungry and forego food? It's something worth contemplating!

When your business is thriving or when you have a substantial salary, especially during times of robust inflow, you may not pay much attention to your expenses. Consequently, you might develop a system where your expenses heavily rely on your active income. Shifting this mindset can be initially challenging because you've grown accustomed to having an open-ended expenses account. It's essential to establish two or three avenues where you can accumulate funds for easy withdrawal during extreme need. This approach will help ensure the financial security of your family. The philosophy of not intermingling personal and professional finances has its roots in earlier times when households had a practice of segregating expenses and setting funds aside for each specific need. They understood that pooling everything together often led to careless spending. Similarly, create distinct reserves to cater to your individual requirements, allowing you to focus on one aspect without being tempted to dip into the other until the need arises.

Another crucial point to recognize is that while you're performing exceptionally well, money is flowing into your household, providing comfort to everyone. However, as we discussed earlier, it's unwise to assume that your income will be perpetual. The day you're unable to bring in sufficient income, your family may have to make compromises due to the shortfall. Therefore, while you're earning well today, it's essential to focus on nurturing your savings, as you can only save money when you have income to save. To ensure you're saving adequately, you can apply the financial thumb rule of setting aside 30% of your monthly income.

The corpus you build while saving consistently will help you take care of your basic needs even during uncertain times when your business is making a loss or your salary is not received on time. Several external factors can put a halt to your active income. Clearly distinguish between the two so that you do not allow either of them to encroach on the other.

Now, when you've established a clear distinction, both your personal and professional life may appear to be in need at times. There will be moments when the temptation to address both will perplex you. There will also be instances when you have to make choices between the two because they both require attention, money, and effort. Without knowing which one to prioritize, there's a risk of a severe imbalance.

"In order to draw a line between the two, you can seek guidance from your financial coach, who will help you identify and prioritize between them. Another effective approach is to create a concrete list of all the major expenses and life milestones that will require financial resources. This way, you can be financially prepared for upcoming events well in advance. Once you've completed the list, you'll be in a better position to segregate the two effectively. Also, ensure you don't lump all your money together in one place."

Only when you "create a firewall between your business liabilities and personal responsibilities" will you be able to effectively manage your finances and life. Failing to do so can result in suffering for either one.

In the next part of this book, you will learn how to strengthen your relationship with each of your sources of income.

Key takeaways from this chapter:

- Depending heavily on active income to cover personal expenses can be risky.

- Creating a clear distinction between your personal and professional life is essential for balance.

- Always have a backup plan for managing your personal finances effectively.

- Overreliance on business income or salary can lead to financial troubles in the future.

- Assuming your income is perpetual can result in overspending from your active income.

Make a list of your personal expenses that can be controlled or budgeted.

CHAPTER 17

STRENGTHEN YOUR RELATIONSHIP WITH MONEY

TRUTH BOMB

Do you prefer a plate of food slammed in front of you in anger or one served to you with love? The same principle applies to money.

Anger and love are two entirely contrasting yet potent emotions. Naturally, most people would prefer love. The same principle applies to money. The law of attraction, the power of visualization, and the "do good to receive good" theory also apply to money. Just like any other relationship, your money benefits from your love and care.

If you think that mastering the realm of personal finance is solely achieved through understanding its IQ (intelligence quotient), you're only scratching the surface. IQ accounts for merely 20% of financial knowledge, while the remaining 80% resides in exploring the EQ (Emotional Quotient) and SQ (Spiritual Quotient) aspects of finance. According to multiple studies, individuals with a high EQ related to money tend to earn three times more than those with lower EQ. A heightened EQ significantly amplifies your ability to attract wealth.

"If IQ were the sole factor in growing wealth, there would be many more affluent individuals." The primary determinant of achieving financial peace is unwavering emotional discipline. The core of EQ is rooted in self-awareness and recognizing that your thoughts and emotions regarding money influence your actions toward it.

'Therefore, EQ + IQ + SQ = Money Mastery'.

This chapter will exclusively concentrate on your connection with money. However, before we delve into comprehending your relationship with money, it's crucial to grasp how it has been shaped thus far. Many of your emotions concerning money are rooted in childhood memories. Each time you exhibit a particular behavior with money, you unconsciously create a pattern that eventually becomes a habit. Your objective should be to enhance your Money EQ to facilitate improved communication and compassion, as this can significantly impact your ability to make prudent financial decisions.

The four major aspects of money are directly tied to your relationship with it:

1. Attract

    The strength and positivity of your relationship with money directly correlate with the amount of money you can draw into your life. This attraction can lead to significant business opportunities and successful collaborations with multinational corporations. As an observation, when encountering affluent individuals, take a moment to consider their relationship with money.

2. Save

    Your intention and commitment to saving will undoubtedly align with having structured financial goals, but you can only save more when you earn more.

3. Multiply

    Although money multiplication follows the magic of compounding, when money realizes it is in good hands, it wants to stay, be pampered, and multiply in those hands.

4. Enjoy

    Only those who are happy and at peace in their lives can truly appreciate the value of money. Individuals surrounded by stress, worries, and burdens are often susceptible to negative emotions related to money.

If you're pondering, "Will this actually work for me?" Rest assured, all four aspects of money will favor you if you cultivate a meaningful relationship with it.

"Use money as a reward, not as therapy." - Anonymous

Several factors contribute to your EQ (Emotional Quotient) with money. In this chapter, my aim is for you not only to assess your current EQ but also to find inner peace with it as you embark on the journey to enhance your relationship with money.

1. "Blessed Money and Cursed Money"

   There is a significant amount of drama surrounding money, and you may frequently encounter individuals lamenting how challenging it is to acquire wealth, while losing it appears effortless. The typical sentiments associated with blessed money encompass joy, empathy, tranquility, satisfaction, well-being, and positive relationships. If you find yourself experiencing these emotions, you are in possession of blessed money in your life. Additionally, your most commendable attributes may involve providing financial assistance to others and displaying generosity when it comes to money.

   However, should you frequently encounter feelings of shame, guilt, fear, anger, regret, and frustration in the context of money, it suggests that you have cursed money in your life. This signifies that your relationship with money may not be very robust, and it becomes imperative to focus on improving it in order to attract a more abundant flow of wealth into your life.

2. Past Money Injuries

   Money blockages are directly linked to your past financial wounds. Have you recently missed out on opportunities for a salary increase or a lucrative project deal? Past family experiences, such as witnessing financial scarcity during childhood, ongoing family disputes due to a lack of funds, job loss, or business setbacks, can negatively impact your relationship with money. Over time, your mind forms a belief that money is inherently bad and evil. This programming grows stronger with each passing day until it becomes natural for you to view money as your worst enemy. Unknowingly, you weaken your connection with money and hinder the flow of wealth into your life.

3. Size of Your Money Vessel

> The larger the size of your money vessel, the more money you can attract. Conversely, with a smaller vessel, you tend to attract less money. This size is directly correlated with your relationship with money. Regardless of the rain's intensity, if you have only a spoon, you'll collect just a spoonful of water. If you possess a glass, your collection will be a glassful, and if you have a bucket, you'll gather a bucketful. However, by implementing the technique of rainwater harvesting, you can ensure access to water throughout the year.

4. Shift of Focus from "Money" to "Life"

> When you're aware that your money is working for you, your central focus in life transitions from the pursuit of money to the enjoyment of life itself. As you engage in living life to the fullest and savoring its experiences, the attainment of an abundant flow of money naturally becomes a byproduct, subsequently enhancing your relationship with money.

The reason why many people struggle to improve their relationship with money is that they are often unaware that something like this even exists. They become deeply engrossed in concentrating solely on the intellectual aspect (IQ) of money, mistakenly believing that mastering money merely involves mastering the financial intellect.

Now that you are acquainted with the concept of the 80% Money EQ theory, your focus should be directed towards enhancing your Money EQ, leaving the domain of Money IQ to the experts. Strengthening your relationship with money is a personal endeavor, while there are individuals available to manage the intricacies of Money IQ on your behalf. The SQ of money places its emphasis on the higher energies that facilitate aligning your relationship with money.

"Money is a result of Emotional, Intelligence and Spiritual Quotient. Understand and unlock your smooth and easy money flow by balancing all the three quotients"

– Deepak Dhabalia.

Let's now explore how to uncover your money personality.

Key takeaways from this chapter:

- IQ comprises only 20% of money mastery, with the significant portion (80%) being attributed to EQ and SQ.

- Your relationship with money predominantly influences the four facets of money: Attract, Save, Multiply, and Enjoy.

- Strengthening your connection with money is essential to attract an abundant flow of wealth into your life.

- Belief in higher energies can also enhance your relationship with money.

- When it comes to Money IQ, it's advisable to let professionals take care of it while you concentrate on Money EQ and SQ.

1.   Write 10 things that money can accomplish for you.

2.   Write 5 positive attributes of money which will strengthen and improve your relationship with money.

CHAPTER 18

DISCOVER YOUR MONEY PERSONALITY*

TRUTH BOMB

Money is a good slave but a poor master.

Now that you are totally confident that your savings and investment journey will get a head start, your relationship with money is now strong, you are sure to build your own money tree... lets now see how you can discover your money personality.

Francis Bacon put it eloquently: "Money is a great servant but a bad master." If used correctly, it can work wonders, but if not, it can destroy lives. When your money is working for you, it's a great servant. However, if you keep working endlessly just to earn money, it can enslave you in chains of gold.

Do these questions bother you at times?

- "Why can't I hold onto money?"

- "Why am I always in a money crisis?"

- "Why do I feel bad when money is going out of my pocket?"

- "Why do some people have an abundant flow of money while some struggle with survival too?"

Each question has the exact same answer to it -

Your money personality determines whether you are a slave to money or a master of money. To ascertain which one predominantly characterizes you, please take the quiz provided below. Choose one of the two options given based on what best describes your behavior.

I shop more than usual during mega sales.

A – No, I plan according to my shopping budget.

B – Yes, I love shopping more during sales.

What does money mean to you?

A – Power, prestige, pride, and an important resource.

B – Anxiety, conflict, worry, and guilt.

What are your financial objectives?

A – Becoming financially independent and being at peace with money.

B – Clearing my debts and earning enough to match my expenses.

Do you believe in Money Multiplication?

A – Truly. It helps to achieve financial freedom.

B – I don't know what Money Multiplication is.

Do you believe that money comes from hard work?

A – No, money comes to me easily.

B – Obviously, money comes only through hard work. I have seen my family work really hard for it too.

What do you do in cases of financial emergency?

A – Pull some money out from my 'emergency fund' piggy bank that I have been saving money into.

B – Try funding it through my current income.

Does planning for your retirement hold significance for you?

A – Yes, becoming financially independent is my primary goal.

B – No, I am never going to retire.

Today is the last day of the month. What is your most likely condition?

A – I still have enough money in my bank account to fund my expenses.

B – I am running out of money. I am waiting to receive my salary tomorrow.

Choose the most likely option amongst the two.

A – Abundant flow of money.

B – A life without EMIs.

What are your views about credit cards?

> A – I do not use a credit card often. I prefer paying my bills through a debit card to avoid overdue payments.

> B – I find the need to use a credit card to keep up with my expenses.

It's time for you to total up your 'As' and 'Bs'.

If most of your answers are A, you are the "Master of Money." You believe in making money work for you because you recognize it as a valuable servant.

However, if most of your answers are B, you are a "Slave of Money." Your mindset leads you to believe that money solely comes from hard work.

Be it the Master or Slave of money, make peace with it. You always have time to rework on it, improvise it once you know what a money personality is and what are its types.

> **"Money is a new form of slavery, distinguishable from the old simply by the fact that it is impersonal - that there is no human relation between master and slave."**
>
> **– *Leo Nikolaevich Tolstoy***

Your money personality shapes your behavior with money, constructs your perception of it, and mirrors your attitudes and characteristics in how you handle money. The development of your money personality is significantly influenced by the money personalities of the people closest to you and your past experiences with money. There are nine money personalities that can either place you in the role of a slave to money or make you its master. As you read through each one, take a moment to relate and contemplate your dominant money personality.

Here are the descriptions of the nine money personalities:

1. Conservative

    If you avoid getting into debt, understand the value of money, and carefully consider significant purchases, it indicates that you have a 'conservative' approach to money. You prioritize a peaceful life over a lavish one.

2. Security Seeker

    If you practice saving before spending, avoid taking risks in your investments, and prioritize your financial security, you exhibit the traits of a 'security seeker'.

3. Money Multiplier

    You believe in making money work for you and are prepared to take the necessary risks to multiply your money. You have a balanced approach, combining both conservatism and a desire for security.

4. Ignorant

    If your approach to money is very casual and you feel it's unimportant to plan your finances, you might be considered 'ignorant' when it comes to your money. However, you are good-hearted, emotional, genuine, and not greedy with your finances.

5. Worrier

    If you often find yourself worrying about your spending, savings, and investments, you fall into the category of a 'worrier.' You have a tendency to feel that money might slip through your fingers, even when there's no compelling reason to be concerned.

6. Avoider

   If you refrain from discussing your finances, blindly entrust their management to someone else, and avoid participating in financial decision-making, you can be classified as an 'avoider' in matters concerning money.

7. Extravagant

   If spending lavishly is your top priority, if you get an instant rush when you spend a lot of money, and if you feel valued when you spend money, you are an 'extravagant.'

8. Debtor

   Despite having less money in your bank account, you proceed to fund your needs and luxuries through loans. If you currently have too many EMIs and feel comfortable taking out loans, you can be categorized as a 'debtor.'

9. Assumer

   If you assume your income to be perpetual, expecting your business or job to provide financial support indefinitely, you fall into the category of an 'assumer' when it comes to money.

The first three personalities – Conservative, Security Seeker, and Money Multiplier – hold the potential to empower you as the master of your finances. However, if you persist in exhibiting the other six personality traits, you will ultimately find yourself entangled in a financial mess, becoming a slave to money.

People often believe that one's personality cannot be altered, but it is possible to consciously change one's money personality.

* The concept of the 9 money personalities is inspired by Ken Honda.

Key takeaways from this chapter:

- Your financial behavior significantly influences your personal financial well-being.

- Engaging in extravagant spending, accumulating excessive loans, and assuming perpetual active income can lead to becoming financially enslaved.

- Strategic spending, adequate savings, and judiciously taking calculated risks to grow your wealth can help you become the master of your finances.

- There are 9 distinct money personalities. Discover your dominant money personality by taking the quiz provided in this chapter.

1.   Currently, are you a slave of money or the master of money?

2.   Identify your dominant money personality.

CHAPTER 19
CHOOSE YOUR CIRCLE WISELY

TRUTH BOMB

Misery attracts company and so does money. Choose your company with caution!

You can now readily identify your own money personality. What's next? Choosing your circle wisely...

Individuals who are unhappy and feel miserable often seek to spread their unhappiness to others. Those who are consistently unhappy may find some consolation in knowing that they are not alone in their feelings. A miserable person can be a formidable force that can bring you down with them.

Just as the saying goes, "you cannot hang out with negative people and expect to live a positive life," similarly, you cannot anticipate your emotions regarding money to be positive and empowering if you surround yourself with people who hold pessimistic views about it.

"Draw a circle around yourself – invite people in or keep them out. We are the creators of our social geometry. Calculate your volume."

– Rachel Wolchin

The same principle applies to money. The individuals you surround yourself with, those who hold the power to influence you, and those with whom you have close interactions all play a significant role in shaping your overall perspective on money. As the saying goes, "you are the sum of the five people closest to you." Therefore, choose your financial influences wisely!

Every Hindi movie from the 90s serves as evidence that the statement above holds true. Most of these stories center around the protagonist getting lured into bad company, leading to a life of recklessness, squandering money, neglecting savings, and failing to provide for their family. Instead, you witness them indulging in lavish and unnecessary parties, and even if they wish to reform, their friends often encourage them not to do so. This theme isn't limited to the realm of cinema; it reflects real-life situations as well. You may be familiar with numerous individuals, possibly even yourself, who had friends that discouraged them from making the right choices. Whether it pertained to academics, attending classes, participating in competitions, launching a new business, or saving money, these are the same people who would push you to play when you needed to study or coerce you into attending a party when exams awaited you the next day.

The same holds true for money. Money attracts company. Whenever you have money, people are drawn to you because they believe you can enhance their parties and live life on a grand scale. They may forget that you have a purpose, goals, and a focused approach to life. They may overlook the fact that your energy is not centered on immediate enjoyment but on spreading enjoyment over the next several years, with the peak coming when you are older.

"Money and power friends. But it's not you they are friends with - just your money and power."

- Auliq-Ice

Similarly, I've had numerous friends in the past who appeared genuinely surprised and distressed when I expressed my preference not to make extravagant purchases or go shopping because I aimed to save that money. They often teased and ridiculed me, suggesting that I had no reason to worry about spending money since I was born into a well-off family with well-to-do parents. As time passed, these were the same individuals who gradually drifted away from my life.

After many years, I came to the realization that my understanding of the significance of money and my commitment to saving and building a robust personal financial portfolio had transformed me into a very distinct individual compared to them. Even today, I observe some of them still financially reliant on their parents, seeking pocket money from them. I've also witnessed a few of them not having a single penny to spare during dire emergencies, forcing them to borrow money from their family and friends or take out loans.

Choosing which school you attend might not have been your choice, and selecting your parents was beyond your control as well. Likewise, determining which brothers or sisters you'll have in your life will not be your decision. However, choosing your circle is entirely within your control and is a matter of personal choice.

I know what you might be thinking: "How can I choose my circle?"

The criteria for individuals who should be part of your circle include:

1. People who possess the knowledge and skill to earn money.

2. People who earn money through ethical means.

3. People who genuinely value money.

4. People who prioritize spending on needs over extravagant wants and luxuries.

5. People who have a profound respect for money and a strong belief in contributing to society.

Look at your close circle of friends, those you hang out with, enjoy your time with, party with, and converse with. Examine the checklist provided above and assess whether they meet these criteria. If not, it's time to consider changing your circle. If they do, consider yourself among the fortunate few on Earth.

Choosing your circle wisely is crucial because your circle can act as a safeguard against temptations and unwise decisions. They will intervene when you're tempted to make extravagant purchases, reminding you of your larger purpose. Moreover, they will refrain from requesting unnecessary loans from you because they understand the effort you put into saving money for yourself. Even if they do borrow money from you, they will make sure to repay it, recognizing that it comes from your personal savings, and you would have made sacrifices to assist them during that time.

The major challenge you may face in choosing your circle wisely is identifying people who are toxic to you. Even if you can identify them, you might find it difficult to distance yourself from them because they have been a part of your life since childhood, or from your school or college days. I'm sure you know people who are not a positive influence on you, and you wish to cut ties with them, but it just doesn't seem possible.

Sometimes when you decline to participate in their extravagance, they may take offense and think you are arrogant. If you do lend them money and they don't pay it back, the moment you ask for your money to be returned, they may consider you miserly. They might even spread negativity about you for asking for the money back. Do you recall encountering such people in your past or current life?

Keep in mind, don't be afraid to let go of people who don't align with your views on money. At the same time, it's also important that you don't make money your best friend. How can you achieve this balance? We'll explore this in the next chapter.

Key Takeaways from This Chapter:

- Your circle has the power to influence you tremendously.

- People who are adversely affecting you and hampering your growth should not be a part of your life.

- It's important to identify the traits and behavior of the people close to you. Accordingly, you can examine your own behavior around money.

- Not everyone should have access to you. The people who contribute to your growth are welcome, but those who don't should be eliminated if you are serious about your financial well-being.

- The right people will always pull you towards becoming the person of your dreams.

1. Identify 5 people who are a good influence on you.

2. Identify 5 people who are a bad influence on you.

CHAPTER 20
DON'T MAKE MONEY YOUR BEST FRIEND

TRUTH BOMB

Money is cunning, it will make you cunning too.
Money is unkind, it will make you unkind too.
Money is cruel, it will make you cruel too.

A best friend is someone who is loyal to you, supports you in tough times, helps you when you're in need, empathizes with you, and is non-judgmental toward you. However, money doesn't possess these qualities. Money can't be anyone's best friend because it is a fickle entity that can turn out to be a poor companion. Making money your primary focus means you may neglect other important aspects of life. If money becomes the only "friend" you relate to, you risk investing so much time in it that you alienate the people around you.

Don't make your life all about money!

Don't forget to live life to the fullest!

Don't forget to enjoy every moment in your life!

Don't forget to be kind to yourself!

Don't forget to indulge in the beauty of life and experiences!

Just because you're obsessed with money, don't make it your best friend.

Easy money that comes in will go out just as easily. If you don't handle it well, it will slip through your fingers. Basing your entire existence on money and making it the only friend you relate to will dehumanize you. You will no longer remain the person you once were.

As much as money can be a blessing in your life, it can also be a curse. Money has the potential to make you petty, mean, overly cautious, unnecessarily cruel, unkind to people, and even greedy at times. It has the power to make you lose your true personality.

You might strongly disagree with me on the idea that money can be cunning, unkind, or cruel. However, the story I'm going to share with you in this chapter will clearly explain why you shouldn't make money your best friend.

An angel and a devil are chatting among themselves, having fun while discussing mankind. The devil often claims that they rule over humans and have complete power over them. The angel disagrees, arguing that some people are good, kind, generous, and fun-loving. She insists that not everyone in mankind is bad, cruel, or evil, as the devil believes. During this conversation, they challenge each other. The devil says, "Pick any good person from your group, and I can turn him into a bad person." The angel is very confident that the devil will fail at this task, as she has great faith in the people belonging to her community. Nevertheless, she selects one person.

The angel chooses a farmer who is extremely poor, lives with his wife and three children, and is struggling to make ends meet for his family. Despite this, the man is incredibly kind, generous, supportive, respectful toward his wife, and loving toward his children. Even with a lack of money and proper food, he never complains about his circumstances. He is hardworking and maintains a positive outlook on life, taking great care of his family and those around him. Everyone loves and admires him for his helpful and kind nature. Given how content and good-hearted he is, the angel is confident that the devil will lose the bet.

The devil accepts the challenge and observes the farmer's daily routine for a couple of days. He notices that the farmer takes the same route to work every day. Deciding to intervene, the devil places a bag of gold coins in the middle of the farm where the farmer will easily see it on his way to work, and then waits for him to discover it. The very next morning, the farmer notices the bag of gold coins. Worried that someone must have left it there by mistake, he rushes around the farm, asking various people if the bag belongs to them. Everyone denies ownership, and knowing how good and helpful the farmer is—and aware of his constant struggles—everyone suggests that he should take the bag of gold coins home with him. After a long and tiring day, he finally decides to do so.

When he returns home with the bag and tells his wife about it, she excitedly asks him to count the coins. At first, the farmer hesitates, suggesting they wait a few days in case someone comes looking for it.

After three days, he too becomes restless and decides to count the coins with his wife. Together, they count 49 gold coins in the bag. His wife says, "There should be one more. It should be 50, not 49. Let's count again!" They recount the coins three times but still find only 49. The next morning, they hurry to the farm, hoping to find the missing coin, but their search is unsuccessful.

Both the farmer and his wife decide to start saving money to acquire that "one" missing gold coin to make the total 50. Ignoring their existing struggles, they resolve to save money for this purpose. To save more, they cut back on meals, reducing their daily intake from two meals to just one for themselves and their children. On some days, to save even more, they go to sleep without eating or drinking. Not seeing any growth in their savings after a few weeks, they further reduce their meal portions. They begin to turn away neighbors who come asking for help. As they continue this regimen for months, their well-being starts to deteriorate. One of their three children falls ill, but the farmer is reluctant to take him to the doctor, fearing it will diminish his savings. The farmer and his wife begin to fight almost daily, frustrated that they haven't been able to save enough money for the "missing gold coin."

They become so stingy, miserly, and miserable with money that the angel is amazed and looks at the devil. Laughing, the devil states that anyone who becomes overly obsessed with money eventually turns evil.

Thus, don't make money your best friend!

Don't curse yourself for not being able to save that last 1,000 rupees, and don't feel guilty for wanting to treat yourself once in a while. Don't become so engrossed with money that you start to mistreat the people around you who mean so much to you. Instead, be happy and comfortable with what you are able to save.

Money can either bring out the best qualities in you, allowing you to be kind, confident, generous, loving, and comfortable, or it can bring out the worst in you, forcing you to become a horrible person.

Obsession with money, like any other obsession, is an extremely harmful disorder. It neither allows you to see the good in people nor enables you to be good to others. To assess your preoccupation with money, you can take note of some common, unhealthy signs. If you find yourself identifying with any of these signs, it's important to disengage from that obsession.

1. If you talk, walk, sleep, and think about money all the time, you are obsessed with money.

2. If you constantly compare your finances with others, you are obsessed with money.

3. If you stress yourself out all the time over your income and expenses, you are obsessed with money.

4. If you have alienated yourself from your family, friends, and society, you are obsessed with money.

I repeat, don't make money your best friend, because you don't know what it might compel you to do on any given day. Also, don't forget, "Money is GOD." Confused? Read the next and final chapter.

Key takeaways from this chapter:

- Money obsession is a harmful disorder.

- Thinking excessively about money can isolate you from the rest of the world.

- Making money your best friend means you can't see or think about anything other than money.

- Don't become the farmer who lost himself to the bag of gold coins.

- Money is volatile; it can either make you a very good person or an extremely bad one.

1.   Write down an incident where you lost a friend because of money.

2.   What do you think will happen to you if you obsess over money by making it your best friend.

CHAPTER 21

MONEY IS GOD

TRUTH BOMB

Treat money the same way like you will treat your God, with devotion, respect and purity.

Don't make money your best friend. Many people view money as a necessary evil. They condition themselves to believe that money is the root cause of all evil. They assume that money makes people more cruel, arrogant, and terrible. However, this is only because they don't regard money as God.

In our culture, Goddess Lakshmi is considered the divine power for wealth, good fortune, and blessed money. As the wife of Vishnu, Goddess Lakshmi is worshiped as the epitome of money and wealth. Whenever we want to show our commitment to God, we typically make an offering in the form of money.

Money is an evolving symbol of economic value, power, and prestige, and is considered to be exceptionally sacred. Anyone who offends the sensibilities of Goddess Lakshmi by disrespecting money will find that Goddess Lakshmi refuses to stay with such families. In essence, you should treat your money as though it is God.

Every time you use money, do so to improve the lives of people, simply because you love them dearly. Each time you spend money, consider whether you are making the world a better place to live. Whenever you handle money, treat it with the respect it deserves, knowing that it isn't easily obtained. Ensure that you store money carefully and don't misuse it or treat it carelessly. If it were a photograph of a god or some form of divine energy, you would naturally keep it safe. You wouldn't step on it, sleep on it, or sit on it; instead, you would make sure to store it carefully and treat it as sacred.

Especially among younger individuals, money is often handled flippantly. They typically do not treat money with the same reverence they would give to their prayers. Even if you do not believe in the concept of God, consider treating money as if it were your God.

Remember,

God is someone who is generous!

God is someone who is kind!

God is someone who gives you what you want!

God is someone who listens to your prayers!

God is someone who ensures that you live your life, purpose, and dreams to the fullest!

This is what we believe of God.

Don't you think money does the same?

Money does exactly the same thing for you, my friend.

Money gives you the freedom you want!

Money gives you luxury and comfort!

Money allows you to be generous!

Money allows you to live the life of your dreams!

Money allows you to follow your passion!

Money allows you to build something bigger, better, and worthy!

So, if you don't believe in God, consider making money your God!

Once you do that, you will then realize what it is like to worship a God. When you worship either entity, be it God or money, you will realize how deeply it connects to your soul.

You must be wondering, "What will happen if I consider money as GOD? Is it going to make any difference?"

The moment you begin to believe that 'Money is God,' every penny wasted, misused, or given to the wrong hands will hurt you deeply from within. You will feel very strongly about every loss because of your powerful connection with money. If someone around you misuses money, you will feel angry and agitated, just as people do when their

God is insulted. In such cases, they might go to great lengths to defend their beliefs, and it would be the same with money. Your money is sacred, and you must treat it with the reverence it deserves.

The Money Manifestation

Dear Money,

Thank you for coming into my life and making my life easy.

Thank you for always protecting me from the bad.

Thank you for giving me multiple opportunities every day to be generous and kind to others.

Thank you for all the luxuries you have given me.

Please bless me, so that I do not misuse you in any manner.

Please ensure that whatever I use it for, brings happiness and joy to the people around me.

Please ensure that I do not waste it on things that are frivolous, insignificant, irrelevant, cruel or unkind.

Please continue being with me and support me when I am in times of distress.

Key Takeaways from This Chapter:

- Money is not the root cause of all evil.

- Consider money as your God.

- Money multiplies in good hands, while it diminishes in the wrong hands.

- To increase your wealth, believe that 'Money is God.'

- As much as you respect and worship God, you should equally respect money.

Write down your pledge for Money that you will practice daily!